T0354699

Professional Learning Communities and Teacher Enquiry

Evidence-based Teaching
for Enquiring Teachers

Professional Learning Communities and Teacher Enquiry

Evidence-based Teaching
for Enquiring Teachers

Alison Fox and Val Poultney

Routledge
Taylor & Francis Group

LONDON AND NEW YORK

First published in 2020 by Critical Publishing Ltd.

Published 2025 by Routledge
4 Park Square, Milton Park, Abingdon, Oxon OX14 4RN
605 Third Avenue, New York, NY 10017

*Routledge is an imprint of the Taylor & Francis Group,
an informa business*

British Library Cataloguing in Publication Data
A CIP record for this book is available from the British Library

ISBN: 9781912508815 (pbk)
ISBN: 9781041056621 (ebk)

Cover design by Out of House Limited
Text design by Out of House Limited

DOI: 10.4324/9781041056621

Acknowledgements

The authors would like to offer thanks for permission to use copyright material in Chapter 2.

- Table 2a is adapted from Table 1, p 95 originally published in Fox and Wilson (2015) Networking and the Development of Professionals: Beginning Teachers Building Social Capital, *Teaching and Teacher Education*, 47: 93–107.

- Jane McGregor for Figure 2a Representations of the same school from two teachers' perspectives.

- Figure 2b: Moving collegial relationships from independence to interdependence (Figure 1 in Little, 1990, p 512).

- Figure 2c network diagram [source Image:SNA_archtype_networks.jpg] from the wikipage http://wiki.resalliance.org/index.php/4.2_Social_Networks_among_Stakeholders

The case studies in this book are offered with thanks to the following practitioners and academic colleagues. For case studies where no individual or organisation is directly attributed and which draw on the authors' own experience, the authors would like to acknowledge those with whom they have worked, reflections on which have led to the development of the included case studies.

Val would like to give particular thanks to Headteacher Jon Fordham of Transform Trust Nottingham for his involvement and insights into the research which informed the case study in Chapter 3 (Reciprocal leadership).

Thanks to members of the RSA Teaching School Alliance, in particular Matthew Purslow associated with the case study in Chapter 4 (Research and development in a Teaching School Alliance).

Alison would like to give special thanks to members of the HertsCam Network, in particular the HertsCam master's team of Dr David Frost, Dr Sarah Lightfoot, Val Hill, Sheila Ball, Paul Barnett and Emma Payne in forming the basis for the case study reported in Chapter 4 (Teacher-led development work as a form of enquiry).

Haiyan would like to thank all the teachers who contributed data to Chapter 5 (Lesson Study) and whose names and schools have been anonymised. They include teachers from a Beijing primary school and several schools which took part in the Camden-based London Schools Excellence Fund Higher Order Mathematics Lesson Study projects (2013–2017).

In Chapter 6 Geoff would like to thank all the teachers who contributed data which has been quoted anonymously and their schools de-identified. He wishes to acknowledge their valued contributions to the reported projects and therefore to this book.

Alison and Eric would like to offer thanks to members of CollectivED, in particular Professor Rachel Lofthouse, based at Leeds Beckett University for providing the case study in Chapter 7 (A model of a contemporary space in which teachers are both consumers and producers of evidence).

Eric would also like to thank his friends and colleagues Alison Fox, Pete Bradshaw and Christine Wise for their continuing support and encouragement. Eric's robust conversations with Pete in the authoring of a course on practitioner research helped shape his thoughts on what would be included in Chapter 7.

Contents

Meet the series editor, author and contributors

Val Poultney

Val Poultney is the series editor for *Evidence-based Teaching for Enquiring Teachers.* She is a senior lecturer at the Institute of Education, University of Derby, teaching on initial teacher education and postgraduate programmes. Her research interests include school leadership and school governance with a particular focus on how to develop leadership to support teachers as researchers. Her last book, *Evidence-based Teaching in Primary Education*, detailed the ways in which partnership-working could support enquiry and systematic investigation by primary teachers as a powerful model of school improvement.

Alison Fox

Alison Fox is a senior lecturer at the Faculty of Wellbeing, Education and Language Studies at the Open University, UK. After training as a secondary-school science teacher, Alison moved into initial teacher training, her research focusing on beginning teachers including their emergent development as school leaders. Over the last 15 years she has been involved in funded projects by the Department for Education Teaching and Learning Research Programme, the National College for Teaching and Leadership and British Council Pakistan related to teachers' professional development. She supports practitioner enquiry through her master's and doctoral supervision.

Eric Addae-Kyeremeh

Eric Addae-Kyeremeh is a senior lecturer in education at the Open University, UK. His teaching primarily focuses on leadership and management in education and he has led and contributed to several Open University master's courses. Eric has worked extensively with teachers and school leaders in the UK, Ghana, India and Bangladesh on a range of development projects. His research interests are broadly in teachers' and headteachers' professional learning across cultures and contexts. His current research focuses on the use of network ethnography to explore 'informal professional learning' among headteachers in Ghana.

Geoff Baker

Geoff Baker is headteacher of Cansfield High School in Wigan and a National Leader of Education. In his current role he has already successfully led the school through an Ofsted inspection that saw its judgement improve to Good. In his previous role as principal of Cromer Academy the school enjoyed year-on-year improvements in every headline measure and the progress of students put it in the top 5 per cent nationally. He has held a number of prestigious fellowships, including a Churchill Fellowship during which he visited schools in Finland and Hong Kong to observe the role of professional communities and explore their part in teacher development. Geoff has published widely in the fields of history and education, with a focus on professional learning communities.

Haiyan Xu

Haiyan Xu worked as a primary English language teacher for several years in China before coming to the UK. In those years, she was routinely involved in Lesson Study activities with colleagues in her school and school district, an experience that significantly shaped her learning and development journey as a teacher. She took opportunities to undertake doctoral studies, investigating the efficacy of Lesson Study as a mode of professional learning and practice development in both the UK and China. Since then she has worked on London Schools Excellence Funds  projects promoting Lesson Study–based communities of practice across various London boroughs. She also tutors on the MSc Educational Leadership and MA International Education courses at the University of Leicester.

Chapter 1
Introduction

Alison Fox

1.1 Chapter overview

This chapter will outline:

1.2   the aims of the book;

1.3   a rationale for the focus on professional learning communities and teacher enquiry;

1.4   the main lines of argument about the benefits of and challenges to teachers' collaboration and enquiry;

1.5   the scope and content of the book;

1.6   questions to initiate a review of enquiry in your setting.

1.2 The aims of this book

This book offers a critically reflective and practical guide to support the development of collaborative teacher enquiry for school improvement, drawing on evidence about teacher collaboration. It aims to promote critical thinking by:

- presenting evidence and counter-evidence through lines of argument;

- considering underlying principles and their links with actions;

- supporting consideration of how the evidence is often context-specific;

- guiding deliberation leading to practical actions.

Professional Learning Communities and Teacher Enquiry as part of the book series *Evidence-based Teaching for Enquiring Teachers* provides a critical overview of different ways of thinking about professional learning as a social process through collaborative and collective activity. These conceptualisations are illustrated through their application in a range of international settings to allow a critical examination of the opportunities and challenges they present to teachers and school leaders. Case studies offer insights into the way the factors affecting collaborative professional learning play out in particular contexts. The book identifies practical recommendations about how to facilitate and engage with collaborative teacher enquiry, based on published evidence. Chapters weigh up the benefits and challenges of the approaches covered and suggest either actions or questions for those of you as readers wishing to act on them in your setting. The book concludes with support for action planning, which includes evaluation of the success of interventions initiated.

1.3 Why focus on professional learning communities and teacher enquiry?

From rhetoric and theorisation about how teachers might develop practice together, there is now increasing evidence about what this means in reality (eg Ofsted, 2018). The complexity of how to support collaborative teacher enquiry has become increasingly apparent, with a number of key factors revealed. There is a message for school leaders about the vision and the structural and cultural leadership needed to unleash teacher agency for school improvement. There is also a message for teachers to hear from other teachers about their experiences of collaborative teacher enquiry.

Recognising the external context

Evidence-based teaching (for more on evidence-based teaching, please see the Afterword on page 109) is an increasingly established part of the discourse of educational improvement by policymakers and educationalists (researchers and teacher educators), with what has been termed 'close-to-practice' enquiry promoted as a mechanism for school (and indeed educational system) improvement (eg Hargreaves, D, 2011; Wyse et al, 2018). Policy references to evidence-based teaching are articulated in the *Carter Review of Initial Teacher Training* (DfE, 2015), the Education white paper *Educational Excellence Everywhere* (DfE, 2016a) and Department for Education (DfE)-commissioned reports (eg Goldacre, 2013a). Organisations and associations now compile and curate evidence about effective continuing professional development to teachers, for example the Education Endowment Foundation (EEF), the Chartered College of Teaching, the Sutton Trust, the EPPI-Centre and the Teacher Development Trust.

Nationally funded studies such as 'Closing the Gap' (Churches, 2016) and 'What makes great CPD for great pedagogy? (Nelson et al, 2015a, 2015b), with whom the book authors have been associated, have contributed evidence about different methods of joint professional development (JPD) (including Lesson Study (LS) and professional learning communities (PLCs)). In a move to build a self-sustaining school system generating evidence to inform practice, the government now funds a growing network of Research Schools (https://researchschool.org.uk) tasked with leading networked research.

These complement the established Teaching Schools (www.gov.uk/guidance/teaching-schools-a-guide-for-potential-applicants; https://tscouncil.org.uk/) who, working as part of Alliances, also have teacher professional development, school-to-school support and research and development (R&D) as part of their 'Big 6' remit. More informally, ResearchED a grassroots evidence-based movement has emerged (https://researched.org.uk) to help disseminate evidence directly to those in the profession.

1.4 The benefits of and challenges to teacher collaboration and enquiry

In these sections of the book, arguments for teachers' collaboration and enquiry are situated to the left of the page, with counterarguments highlighting the challenges situated to the right.

> **Teachers are being challenged to refocus on enhancing children's learning, rather than on their teaching, so taking a greater responsibility for progressing students' learning outcomes. This need not be tackled in isolation. Rather, teachers should consider their responsibility a collective one which should be taken on as a collective, as a professional learning community.**

(DuFour and Eaker, 1998)

> **Teachers are used to working in isolation due in part to their busyness but also to the cultures and structures in place in a school, which holds them accountable for the students they teach directly. Teachers like to work independently to allow them a sense of ownership over their practice, and to be creative in ways they feel best placed to determine as might benefit their students.**

(Achinstein, 2002; Hargreaves, A, 1994; Little, 1990)

> **Even if we agree to focus on improving students' learning and drawing on the perspectives of others, how do teachers know which practices are effective, which to change and which are worth trying? Teachers need an evidence base to draw upon. But should such evidence be developed from local enquiry or adopted and adapted from published research? Both are powerful sources towards evidence-informed practice.**

(Stenhouse, 1983; Elliott, 1980; Cain et al, 2016; Philpott and Poultney, 2018)

> **It is really hard to retain staff and partners in climates of unstable funding and high workloads so, whenever there are efforts towards gaining a consensus on a vision, staff leave and the process of getting everyone on board starts again. The constant restarts cause intervention overload on staff who are less likely to take the next expectation of them on board.**

(Clement, 2013)

> **If educational leaders see the value of enquiry and of collaboration, they will create the cultures and structures to create the times and spaces for teachers to meet. This might be face-to-face or virtually, within their teaching day or beyond.**

(Cordingley, 2008; Hargreaves, A, 1997)

1.5 The scope and structure of this book

Chapter 2 maps the *Language of collaboration and enquiry*. Alison Fox explores the language of social assemblages associated with teacher collaboration, namely teams, communities, networks and partnerships, to contextualise the book's focus on JPD for teacher enquiry. This is referenced against evidence from a range of studies which are set within a research timeline, providing an overview of the development of ideas and evidence base associated with these alternative ways to conceptualise teacher collaboration and enquiry. The chapter concludes with possible actions and further resources for use in school settings.

School–university partnerships as contexts for enquiry form the focus for Chapter 3, in which Val Poultney explores the complexities of engaging in such partnerships. This chapter engages with the evidence for the benefits of and opportunities afforded by such partnerships, while acknowledging the challenges. Practical advice is offered about what to consider when engaging in partnerships for school improvement and ways forward explored through case studies.

In Chapter 4 about *Teacher-led enquiry*, Alison Fox offers a characterisation of different forms of such enquiry: informal-formal; individual-collaborative. This is set in the UK political context that schools are increasingly expected to provide school-based evidence to inform practice development when there is a reduced funding stream to support teacher- and school-led enquiry. Contemporary case studies are included for concrete illustrations of the issues.

Haiyan Xu focuses on *Lesson Study* in Chapter 5 as a particular form of joint enquiry/professional development. The chapter draws on an international review of published work covering approaches to and evidence arising from Lesson Study internationally and on the work of this author with Pete Dudley, who is considered responsible for bringing Lesson Study into England and Wales. Different variants of Lesson Study are compared and contrasted. Issues associated with carrying out Lesson Study are illustrated with vignettes from England and China. The chapter concludes with key actions for those who want to adopt this form of collaborative enquiry.

Geoff Baker focuses in Chapter 6 on the notion of *professional learning communities (PLCs)*, introduced in Chapter 2. The chapter examines two alternative practical applications aimed at PLC-building, unpacking how visions are balanced against the challenges of putting these into practice. Advice is illustrated through case studies in two English educational settings from the author's own close-to-practice enquiry. This is designed to help school leaders appreciate the possible implications of alternative approaches to developing PLCs.

Chapter 7 by Eric Addae-Kyeremeh focuses on *Teachers' access to evidence*. This outlines the range and forms of evidence to which teachers have access and argues that evidence-based practice requires teachers to be critical readers of published work. It raises challenges for applying findings from academic studies to teachers' contexts without critical examination of context, scope and scale. The chapter concludes with reflections on how, while traditional academic educational research has been difficult to access by teachers, there are new ways to engage across professional and academic boundaries, for example using social networking for teachers' professional learning. Case studies illustrating different ways teachers can access evidence are included.

The book concludes with Chapter 8, *Conclusions and take-aways,* in which Alison Fox brings together the evidence base for key claims made in the book about PLCs and teacher enquiry. The chapter summarises practical advice for: choosing which form of collaborative enquiry to adopt; those leading collaborative enquiry and those engaging with such enquiry. It concludes with a framework for building on the actions and key questions identified to support reader action planning, which is a key feature of the *Evidence-based Teaching for Enquiring Teachers* book series.

1.6 Summary

The authors hope you find this an accessible, topical and supportive resource for your work in and with schools, whatever your role, through the theoretical and practical advice drawn from evidence-based sources. We hope readers will share this resource with those who are joining the profession through any of the current initial teacher education routes, in support of developing an evidence-informed and empowered profession. While this book draws mainly on school-based research and refers to 'teacher' enquiry, school can be read as any other educational setting/organisation and teacher interpreted as educator (teaching assistant, adviser, specialist consultant etc).

Questions for enquiry in your own school

Using the outcomes of the national UK study 'What makes great CPD for great pedagogy? (Stoll et al, 2012b), the following questions can act as a checklist to help plan for effective collaborative professional development through enquiry in your educational setting. If you are not in a position to drive such strategy, you could use these questions to engage with your setting's leadership.

- To what extent does your setting already operate collaboratively both within and beyond the organisation?

- Does the setting have a way of assessing individual and school needs in order to use this analysis to drive enquiry?

- Does a culture exist that accepts that, for professional development to be effective in changing practice, it needs to challenge current thinking?

- Do existing structures and processes involve educators in connecting work-based learning with external expertise?

- Does the organization have a long-term strategy which involves professional learning opportunities for educators which are varied, rich and sustainable?

- Is your setting's strategy one which uses practitioner enquiry as its key tool?
- Is everyone clear of the desired outcomes for enquiry?
- Are the setting's leadership aware of the challenges and opportunities for creating the necessary conditions for collaborative enquiry?

Chapter 2
Mapping the language of collaboration and enquiry

Alison Fox

2.1 Chapter overview

This chapter will outline:

2.2   key questions relating to the language of teacher collaboration and enquiry;

2.3   a summary timeline of key ideas associated with teacher collaboration and enquiry;

2.4   key arguments relating to the language of teacher collaboration and enquiry;

2.5   definitions of a team and how these relate to teacher collaboration;

2.6   forms of community and their relationships to teacher collaboration and enquiry;

2.7   definitions of a network and networking and how teachers can network effectively;

2.8   alternative notions of collective useful for thinking about teacher collaboration and enquiry – sets and partnerships.

This chapter covers the development of an evidence base about the benefits and challenges of thinking about different assemblages of teachers involved in collaboration and enquiry: in teams; communities; networks; sets and partnerships. It points to practical implications of these ideas for those in schools leading and involved in teacher collaboration and enquiry.

2.2 Key questions relating to the language of teacher collaboration and enquiry

The language related to forms of collaboration is rich and potentially confusing. This chapter addresses the following questions with reference to empirical studies and reviews of published literature around teacher collaboration and enquiry.

- What are the definitions of a: team; community; network; set and partnership and how do they relate to one another?

- What forms of collective are there in relation to teachers working collaboratively and engaging in enquiry?

- How do different ways of thinking about teacher connectivity differ and what do they contribute to thinking about professional development and school improvement?

- What practical applications arise from thinking about different forms of teacher collaboration and enquiry?

2.3 A summary timeline of key ideas associated with collaboration and enquiry

The timeline below presents a chronology of key ideas informing the language of teacher collaboration and enquiry covered in this book.

Timeline of key ideas

1930s

★ Reflective practice: Dewey (1933)

1960s

★ Teachers as researchers: Stenhouse (1968, 1975, 1981, 1983); Elliott (1980)

★ Discovery learning: Bruner (1961)

1970s

• The strength of weak ties: Granovetter (1973, 1983)

1980s

★ US based reforms around teacher community: cited in Achinstein (2002)

★ The reflective practitioner: Schön (1984)

1990s

★ The learning organisation: Senge (1990)

★ The knowledge-creating company: Nonaka and Takeuchi (1995)

★ The persistence of privacy: Little (1990)

* Communities of practice: Lave and Wenger (1991); Wenger (1998)

* A typology of school cultures: Andy Hargreaves (1994)

* School–university partnerships as centres of pedagogy: Goodlad (1994), Johnstone and the Educators for Collaborative Change (1997)

* Extended professionalism: Cochran-Smith and Lytle (1993, 1999)

* The value of social capital: Putnam (1995)

* Knotworking: Engeström, Engeström and Vähäaho (1999)

* Networks for educational change: Lieberman and McLaughlin (1992)

* PLCs: Hord (1997); DuFour and Eaker (1998); Lieberman and Miller (2001)

2000s

* The network-centred society: Castells (2000); Rainie and Wellman (2012)

* NetWORKers and intensional networks: Nardi, Whittaker and Schwarz (2000, 2002)

* Communities of enquiry/Enquiry communities: Cochran-Smith and Lytle (2009); Levine (2010); Pardales and Girod (2006)

* The importance of teacher teamwork: Krammer, Rossmann, P, Gastager, A and Gasteiger-Klicpera (2018); McEwan, Ruissen, Eys, Zumbo and Beauchamp (2017); Park, Henkin and Egley (2005); Young (2006)

* From PLC to Networked Learning Communities: Jackson and Temperley (2006)

* The impact of PLCs: Vescio, Ross and Adams (2008)

* Digital teacher networks: Schlager, Farooq, Fusco, Schank and Dwyer (2009)

* Networking practitioner research: McLaughlin, Black-Hawkins, McIntyre with Townsend (2007)

2010s

* The self-improving school system: David Hargreaves (2010, 2011)

* 'What works' culture: Hattie (2008, 2012), Education Endowment Foundation (2017, 2019)

* Sets and nets: Dron and Anderson (2014a, 2014b)

* Landscapes of practice: Wenger-Trayner, Fenton-O'Creevy, Hutchinson, Kubiak and Wenger-Trayner (2015)

2.4 Key arguments relating to the language of teacher collaboration and enquiry

In the following illustrations of the arguments levied for (to the left) and against (to the right) teacher collaboration, key terms for different assemblages of teachers are highlighted in italics and are examined further in this chapter.

When we (school leaders) want a task completing and want to distribute the work, we often use *teams,* schedule work to be completed and set monitoring points. Not only does this share the workload but it also gets colleagues on board by feeling empowered as part of the developments.

(Leithwood et al, 2008; Dionne et al, 2004)

Self-selecting teams have been shown not necessarily to be as impactful to developing practice and improving pupils' learning outcomes as leader-orchestrated *teams*, but are less liked by teachers. Should colleagues be put together on the basis of complementary skills, accepting that support might be needed?

(Young, 2006; McEwan et al, 2017; Hakkarainen et al, 2004)

School leaders often talk about developing *community* as part of a school's ethos. It is therefore accepted that teachers should support one another for the benefit of the students for whom they have professional responsibility, while also learning themselves as part of continuing professional development.

(Grossman et al, 2000)

What makes a *community*, rather than just a group of teachers? Teachers, as in other walks of life, can be seen to spend time and work together but not actually progress their practice in meaningful ways

(Levine, 2010; Grossman et al, 2000; Little, 1990)

> Thinking about practice is an important part of a *community*, whether a *community of practice* or a *professional learning community*. Welcoming newcomers into those practices is also a feature. If collaborative enquiry is something leaders want to emphasise, *communities of enquiry* could also be useful to think about.

(Bolam et al, 2005; DuFour and Eaker, 1998; Lave and
Wenger, 1991; Levine, 2010; Lieberman and Miller, 2001)

> *Communities* highlight working in close proximity to one another and developing shared repertoires of practice. However, this raises the danger of practices becoming ossified as a result of 'group think' if there is no re-energisation from new ideas or challenge from fresh perspectives.

(Evans et al, 2006; McCormick et al, 2010; Wenger, 1998)

> *Communities* of which teachers are members are only one social assemblage in which teachers can work together and collaborate. Wider possibilities for teacher interactivity with sources of knowledge, advice, inspiration and challenge to their thinking, can be represented as their *networks. Networking* can be an active way of building, maintaining and reactivating aspects of a network. In the contemporary digitally networked world, the potential others and ways of interacting are almost unfathomable.

(Dron and Anderson, 2014a; Manca and Ranieri, 2017; McCormick
et al, 2010; Nardi et al, 2000; Rainie and Wellman, 2012).

2.5 What is a team and what does evidence say about teacher teams?

'Team' has origins in the Old Frisian word tām for bridle and Old Norse taumr for chain, linking team to the notion of *yoking animals together*. An established definition of team relevant to the context of teacher collaboration is '*a group of people organized to work together*' (Collins, 2018). Interestingly this British definition, compared with its American equivalent, includes the word 'organised', implying an expectation that teams are not self-initiated but are established by others (presumably those more senior). Teams, at least in the British context, can therefore be argued to be a leadership device to accomplish certain tasks. In other contexts, Krammer et al's study of around 400 teachers working in Austrian teacher teams (2018) showed that self-selected rather than administrative-formed teams reported higher ratings for sharing responsibility in their classroom work. This was inferred to be due to teachers knowing one another well enough to judge with whom they could meaningfully work. However, administration-organised teams rated higher in terms of their effectiveness to make progress in practice development, implying that self-selection does not ensure that the full range of skills necessary for good quality teaching are included within teams.

Teacher teams have the potential to contribute to school improvement and reform, and reinvigorate schools (eg Park et al, 2005), as long as leaders recognise *'the creativity and skills of teachers who willingly contribute their energy and loyalty through collective efforts and teamwork processes'* (Park et al, 2005, p 462). In practice, inertia due to a lack of challenge or open-mindedness can apply to teams, as much as to other relational groupings (Young, 2006). An American study of four schools focusing on how effectively teams used data to inform learning and teaching (Young, 2006) highlighted how important agenda-setting is for teams, especially if normative practices are not already collaborative. Further, those with better external connectivity appeared more aware of the purposes for and accountability of their practices and hence the significance of their teamwork.

Teamwork is therefore not something in which it can be assumed teachers can engage without support. A systematic review of published studies across a wide range of disciplines concluded that training increased the effectiveness of teams, as long as this required members to actively learn about and practise teamwork (McEwan et al, 2017). Thinking about the composition of, support for and ways of working in teams is further explored in relation to a particular form of team teacher collaboration – Lesson Study – in Chapter 5.

2.6 How does the notion of a community relate to teacher collaboration and enquiry?

Community is one of the 1000 most commonly used words in the Collins Dictionary, but its definitions are diverse (Collins, 2018). Community sometimes refers to *'the people living in one locality'* or to *'the locality in which they live'* (Collins, 2018) emphasising either the people or the place. It can be used as a modifier to reflect the implied sense of belonging associated with local engagement, such as in 'community spirit'. Other definitions relate to shared characteristics of a group, other than where they reside, such as cultural, religious or ethnic commonalities. Communities can therefore sit within or extend beyond a particular place. Interconnectedness, collective participation and stability are common themes across definitions of community; all with positive associations.

Following a series of reforms in the USA which promoted teacher community development (Carnegie Task Force, 1986; Rosenholtz, 1989), a number of authors reflected on their success. Judith Warren Little (1990), Hargreaves, A (1994) and Achinstein (2002) challenged whether the interconnectedness and common purpose aspired to by such reforms were being achieved, so generating meaningful collaborative work. Instead, they exposed inertia and silo working as the norms in schools, concluding it was an error for school leaders to assume that, by facilitating teachers to work together, they would become a collaborative community. Little (1990) noted a *'persistence of privacy'* and Hargreaves, A (1994) *'egg-crate'* and *'Balkanised'* cultures. These may be something you recognise even in contemporary schools.

The notion of teacher collegiality, originally defined practically as teachers conferring and collaborating with one another (Smythe, 1991), became politicised within the education sector to mean something more strategic, to democratically share school decision-making among staff and stakeholders (Brundrett, 1998). Interest in how teachers' collegial relationships could develop into teacher communities pointed to the need for appropriate school cultures to be in place, built on mutual trust.

Even if collegial working is accepted as desirable, the limitations of aspiring only to close-knit communities have been raised (de Lima, 2001). This ignores the power of what have been termed 'weak ties', to those beyond the immediate collective (Granovetter, 1973, 1983). Network analysis (covered further in section 2.7) has proved powerful in revealing the evidence and limitations of teachers' relationships if limited to within-school communities and groups (Baker-Doyle, 2011; Carmichael et al, 2006; de Lima, 2007). Departments can have very different collegial relationships from one another, internally and with the rest of the school. These have been shown to affect the extent to which teacher talk and joint work focuses on the development of teaching (de Lima, 2007). This leads to differences in perception of the same school from different teacher perspectives, as illustrated in Figure 2a by examples from a study in which teachers were invited to offer artistic representations of their school. Some departments were perceived as 'no go' areas, even in schools whose leaders had been working explicitly to develop strong school collegiality (McGregor, 2004).

Figure 2a Representations of the same school from two teachers' perspectives

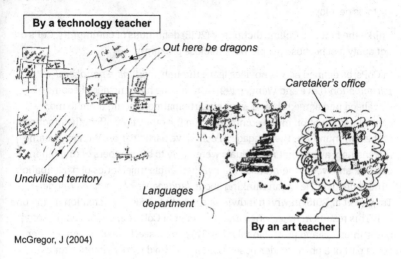

By a technology teacher

Out here be dragons

Caretaker's office

Uncivilised territory

Languages department

By an art teacher

McGregor, J (2004)

These insights confirm that, if community-building is an aspiration, existing school cultures need to be reviewed to identify likely challenges (Baloche and Brody, 2017).

Teacher communities have become multiply conceptualised. This chapter covers four conceptualisations: communities of practice; PLCs; enquiry communities; and communities of learners.

How does the notion of community of practice relate to teachers?

Lave and Wenger (1991) propose a model of learning based on apprenticeship through social participation. This imagines novices joining others engaged in similar practices in what is termed a Community of Practice (CoP). Through participation, individuals form views of who they want to become. These views affect novices' practices and their beliefs about practices, so affecting their identity development and sense of belonging. Three criteria characterise a CoP:

- **mutual engagement** – members must be engaged in some activity together, which contributes to the shared practices of the community;

- **joint enterprise** – practice is shaped by a collective process of negotiation with others engaged in this practice, in ways which are independent of organisational definitions of it;

- **shared repertoire** – over time, through the engagement and enterprise described above, cultural routines, terminology, resources and conceptual tools develop.

Unlike the first two Collins dictionary (2018) definitions of community, CoPs do not apply just because people work in close proximity.

In CoPs, as defined above, novices learn through *'legitimate peripheral participation'* (Lave and Wenger, 1991). On the one hand, novices become socialised into agreed shared ways of participating, leading them to more central participation in the community. On the other, they affect the practices of the community as they engage in collective participation. Wenger became increasingly aware that individuals were likely to be members of more than one CoP and would therefore be following multiple trajectories of participation simultaneously. He began thinking about *'landscapes of practice'* (Wenger-Trayner et al, 2015) in which individuals negotiate their participation in any one CoP. This results in trajectories into a number of CoPs, depending on personal goals, interests and professional roles. This could see, for example, a teacher being part of a phase leader-based CoP (if they hold responsibilities for a particular age group in a school), one or more subject-based CoPs (depending on the teacher's curricular responsibilities) and a leadership CoP (if working on a particular cross- or inter-school strand of work).

So, if CoPs are communities of practitioners, how do they differ from the notion of PLCs, emerging into the language of teacher collaboration around the same time?

How does the notion of a PLC relate to teachers?

PLCs can be traced back to inspiration by John Dewey's (1933) notions of reflective practice, extended by Lawrence Stenhouse and John Elliott in the 1970s and 1980s to school-based development work based on the ideas of *'teacher-as-researcher'* (Bolam et al, 2005), the *'reflective practitioner'* (Schön, 1984) and *'learning organisations'* (OECD, 2016; Senge, 1990). After adopting terminology from the business sector in the 1990s (Hord, 1997; DuFour, 2004; DuFour and Eaker, 1998), PLCs were taken on most progressively in the USA in the 2000s as a mechanism for school reform. They since developed a following through the English-speaking world as part of an international school improvement and effectiveness movement (Hargreaves, A, 2007; Stoll and Louis, 2007). PLCs came into focus in England through a large-scale research project, *Creating and Sustaining Effective PLCs* (Bolam et al, 2005).

Stoll et al refer to the definition of a PLC as the situation:

> **... in which the teachers in a school and its administrators continuously seek and share learning, and act on their learning. The goal of their actions is to enhance their effectiveness as professionals for the students' benefit.**

(Stoll et al, 2006, p 33)

PLCs are termed:

- **professional** because all activity is focused on improving student outcomes through improving teaching practice;

- **learning** by assuming knowledge resides among professionals and their everyday practice;

- **communities** by assuming collaborative learning with peers is their central principle.

The characteristics of effective PLCs include *'shared values and vision; collective responsibility; reflective professional enquiry (eg mutual observation); collaboration; the promotion of group, as well as individual, learning'* (Stoll et al 2006, p 227). Moving teachers from *in*dependence to *inter*dependence (Little, 1990 and Figure 2b) collaboration is challenged to go ... *'beyond superficial exchanges of help, support or assistance'* (Stoll et al 2006, p 227). Little critiques activity, which might at first appear collaborative. For example, recounting classroom 'stories' in staffrooms as offering only affirmation rather than problem-solving. Similarly, teachers asking for tips and resources from one another might be limited to short-term 'aid', sharing limited descriptions of practice rather than challenging and developing practice. A move to a more powerful, interdependent approach to collegiality has been energetically championed by Ann Lieberman and colleagues in the USA and in Canada (Lieberman and Miller, 2001, 2008; Lieberman and Wood, 2002). However, contriving such collegiality needs to accept that the micropolitics of teacher relationships will need to be overcome (Achinstein, 2002; Ball, 2012; Hargreaves, A, 1994).

Figure 2b Moving collegial relationships from independence to interdependence (Figure 1 in Little, 1990, p 512).

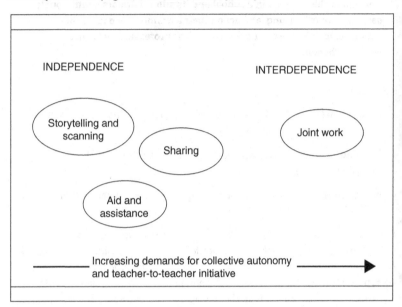

In PLCs the aim is that *'tacit knowledge [is] constantly converted into shared knowledge through interaction'* (Stoll et al 2006, p 227), requiring reflective and collective enquiry. The seminal publication about knowledge-creating companies, emerging from Japanese work by Nonaka and Takeuchi (1995), influenced the field of education in recognising the importance of making knowledge explicit for organisational learning. PLCs have been found to be impactful on student outcomes in a review of US and UK initiatives (Vescio et al, 2008) as well as being positive experiences for the educators involved.

In what other ways can teacher communities be defined?

Recognising the potential for practice within communities to stagnate, Veugelers and O'Hair recommend that PLCs should be outward-looking:

> **PLCs...grow stronger and become more vibrant when they are connected to other learning communities, rather than when they operate entirely alone. The best way to bring this about is through networks.**

(Veugelers and O'Hair, 2005, p ix)

PLCs therefore become 'networked PLCs' (Jackson and Temperley, 2006), a realisation which led to the development and operation in England by the National College of Networked Learning Communities (NLCs) between 2002 and 2006, involving 35,000 staff and over 675,000 pupils. Further discussion of networks and teacher enquiry is covered in 2.7.

Another conceptualisation of community is an 'enquiry community' (Levine, 2010) or 'community of enquirers' (Pardales and Girod, 2006; Garrison et al, 2010). As with PLCs, this is built on notions of 'teachers-as-researchers' (Stenhouse, 1981; Elliott, 1999, 2004). That teachers should base their decision-making on evidence has been termed part of their 'extended professionalism' (Cochran-Smith and Lytle, 1993), which educational leaders and policymakers should value. This recognises teachers as those implementing and developing innovations and hence practice. As enquiry communities, groups of teachers focus on learning from one another through asking questions and searching for answers collectively. Levine (2010) recognises that this concept encompasses a range of collectives which might be known as teacher research communities, teacher research groups (eg Fairbanks and LaGrone, 2006), critical friend groups (eg Curry, 2008) and Lesson Study groups (as examined in Chapter 5). Some forms of enquiry community refer to using particular tools, such as the 'cycle of enquiry' framework (Sagor, 1992) or 'protocol-guided discussions' (Curry, 2008) to provide prompts and scaffolding.

A final noteworthy branch of thinking around communities, traced to Barth (1984), is the notion of a 'community of learners'. First proposed in work with school principals, this later developed into a concept embracing both adult and student learning. While this is arguably the least theorised as to how such communities can be operationalised (Levine, 2010), it highlights the value of students in the learning of their teachers.

Are there limits to thinking about communities?

Three key limitations of CoPs have been identified (Amin and Roberts, 2008; Cornelissen et al, 2006; Evans et al, 2006; Handley et al, 2006; McCormick et al, 2010; Wenger et al, 2002). Firstly, communities meeting CoP criteria (Wenger, 1998) are difficult to identify, with workplaces experienced as more fragmented places of social interaction than easily bounded communities. Secondly, Lave and Wenger's (1991) work is claimed, by focusing on apprenticeship, not to explain the learning of experienced professionals. Thirdly, emphasising a shared repertoire and sets of tools is argued to prioritise current practice and ignore the dangers this presents to developing practice. Instead, newcomers, whether novices or those transferring from other settings, should be considered as bringing useful knowledge and ideas for developing practice, rather than viewing them only as needing to be socialised (Fox and Wilson, 2008).

Similarly, critiques have been made about PLCs. An international review (Servage, 2009) concluded that a school's interpretations of the concept *professional* will be central to the way a PLC is enacted. The aims and practice of communities can be expected to differ depending on whether teachers are viewed as *'scientists; caring moral agents; advocates for social justice or learning managers'*. Our current performative culture favours the latter view and readers might recognise a dominant managerial approach to learning for both teachers and pupils. This is deemed responsible for limiting the scope for deepening teachers' professional development by prioritising performance targets. Servage (2008) argues that school leaders should refocus on the desired ends for PLCs (or presumably any form of community) in order to critically determine appropriate means to enact them.

Levine concluded that, while enquiry communities are useful for collectives explicitly engaged in enquiry, they are less useful for other forms of *'joint work, such as rewriting curriculum together, co-teaching, mentoring, or peer-observing'* (Levine, 2010, p 113).

Finally, it is worth accepting that, in reality, the various forms of community defined in this chapter are likely to *'overlap as teachers engage in multiple and evolving forms of collaborative activity'* (Levine, 2010, p 124). More inclusive, less prescriptive views of teacher interaction and assemblages are notions of networks and networking.

2.7 What is a network and what does networking mean?

Any particular individual's *'network or net'* refers to the people, groups or organisations with whom they connect (or *'nodes'*), the connections between them, and their relationships (as *'links', 'ties', 'edges'* or *'threads'*) (Dron and Anderson, 2014a, 2014b; Rainie and Wellman, 2012; McCormick et al, 2010).

Figure 2c Network mapping revealing simple forms of network structure

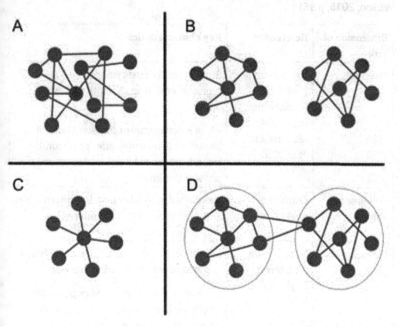

Each person's network is unique and, when combined with others, creates social networks of great complexity. Simple versions of forms from a limited number of nodes are represented in Figure 2c. Seen from an individual's perspective looking outwards, a 'worm's-eye view' (Carmichael et al, 2006), such structures are helpful in describing the resources available to an individual. Nodes can be drawn on for information, advice, collaboration or social support; all vital when thinking about ways educational practitioners can learn from one another. Unlike some of the earlier collectives, networks lack a particular designed structure or concept of membership (Dron and Anderson, 2014b; Rainie and Wellman, 2012; McCormick et al, 2010). They include team-working or community membership as part of a bigger picture, or bird's-eye view, of teacher connectivity. The world wide web and social media, as part of an increasingly *'network-centred society'* (Castells, 2000; Rainie and Wellman, 2012), are further expanding teachers' opportunities to connect with one another and a wide range of others (Fox and Bird, 2017).

The processes associated with initiating, sustaining or reactivating links are termed networking (Nardi et al, 2000). Church et al explain *'threads tie us to each other through our joint activity and create the strength to hold us'* (2002, p 16). Such links can be described in a number of ways (see Table 2a).

Table 2a Dimensions for conceptualising network links (adapted from Fox and Wilson, 2015, p 95)

Dimension of link	References	Key characteristics
Strength	Granovetter, 1973, 1983; Hakkarainen et al, 2004; McCormick et al, 2010.	Strong – individuals work closely and regularly and in an in-depth way with others. Weak – occasional or transient but not to be discounted as they offer opportunities for individuals to be exposed to alternative ways of thinking.
Perceived value	Carmichael et al, 2006.	Associated with advice and/or information and/or emotional support offered by engaging with a node.
Formality	Baker-Doyle, 2011; Baker-Doyle and Yoon, 2011.	Formal – related to structures and systems associated with a practitioner's work. Informal – not pre-planned or put in place by others. Less well studied but potentially important for support.
Temporality	Nardi et al, 2000.	a. The initiation and establishment of links. b. The development and maintenance of these links (or conversely, the lack of their development). c. Re-activation of links to meet particular needs.

The *strength* of a link indicates how much interaction there is between the focal person and others. The perceived *value* of a link relates to how much the focal person feels they get from the relationship with the other. The *formality* of a link refers to whether the resources are associated with formal aspects of their activities, such as through in-service or initial teacher education provision, or through more informal opportunities for networking. *Temporality* refers to how each relationship develops and how proactive the focal person is in utilising these links over time. Describing the nature of a professional's links reveals the mechanisms for gaining effective support.

Nardi et al (2000, 2002) encourage us all to be proactive in our networking, to create *'intensional personal networks'* in which we are conscious and active in the links we make, and with which nodes we interact aware of their purposes. This is described as putting them intentionally in 'tension'. As our personal and professional interests and needs change over time, our networks flux. *'Knots or knotworks'* of particular assemblages can form temporarily to complete a time-dependent project (Engeström et al, 1999; Hakkarainen et al, 2004). This would be an illustration of how part of a network can be activated. Understanding how individuals network (when used as a verb) can help understand, not only why others can be seen as resources for collaboration such as joint enquiry, but how these resources can become accessible (Carmichael, 2011; Carmichael et al, 2006; Fox and Wilson, 2009; McCormick et al, 2010). Some have coined the phrase *'personal learning networks'* (Rajagopal et al, 2012; Richardson and Mancabelli, 2011) to refer to the learning opportunities an individual's personal network affords. Networks might not be as equable and democratic as might appear at first sight and power relationships are evidenced as affecting access to knowledge, who has a voice and who is silenced (eg Robson, 2016). The role of influencers has been recognised in both general (eg Bosworth et al, 2015) and school-to-school networks (eg Muijs et al, 2010).

The development of a landscape of networks of schools and enquiry

The NLCs of the early 2000s were a highly structured attempt to set up networks of schools, and hence their staff who would work together on agreed agendas. These were derived from the seminal work *The Education Epidemic* (Hargreaves, D, 2003) and its description of the value of what were termed *'innovation networks'*, accountable not only to one another but also to the National College. Following this period, as already noted, the Teaching Schools and Teaching School Alliances were established, with responsibilities for leading R&D and school-to-school support. The *'researching school'* became part of the UK lexicon, with key features of such schools identified as:

- a strong emphasis on dialogue and collaboration;

- an emphasis on multi-level or distributed leadership, with a freedom to act for all involved;

- establishing a moral purpose about the need to do things differently on behalf of learners;

- the personal commitment and championing of research by senior leadership;

- the effective co-ordination of small-scale, teacher-initiated enquiries;

- partnership with *higher education institutions* (HEIs), to act as critical friends and facilitators;

- an understanding and acceptance that enquiry needs to be robust and at an appropriate scale to be useful to the professional setting;

- adequate resourcing for the time needed for internal and external collaboration;

- sustained commitment to developing research cultures;

- involving a wide range of voices in the research, including students (McLaughlin and Black-Hawkins, 2004).

The literature review from which this list derives covered three scales: teachers as researchers, schools as researching institutions and networks of researching schools. Written when the NLCs were at their peak presence, it concluded that school-to-school networks were most effective when supported:

a) at school-level – for, and through co-ordination of, teachers' concerns and aspirations;

b) by HEI or other external, research-experienced critical friends – to help maximise the impact of the activities of the schools and networks;

c) by government and national agencies – for financial resourcing and rhetorical encouragement.

Since this time, however, the latter aspect has significantly shifted in the UK. The Department for Education became disillusioned with school-led, usually largely qualitative, enquiry (Goldacre, 2013a, 2013b), even when undertaken by the collective work of Alliances across the country. Its appetite changed to evidence-at-scale, seen as more useful to judge the effectiveness on practice of various interventions and approaches.

Randomised controlled trials (RCTs) (eg Sutton Trust, 2012–2018; EEF, 2019) began to be the predominant form of study commissioned (Philpott and Poultney, 2018). These trials require large numbers of schools as, for any particular trial, participating schools are allocated either a control or experimental role. To help satisfy the demand the Department for Education established a funding stream for a new form of schools' network. Research Schools and the Research School Network were launched in 2017, in parallel to the ongoing Teaching Schools and Teaching School Networks. At the time of writing this book, this Network is collaboratively led by the EEF and the Institute for Effective Education. Initially 11 Research Schools were selected through a competitive application process, with each school receiving £200,000 over three years *'to become focal points of evidence-based practice in their region and build networks between large numbers of schools'* (EEF, 2017). The number of schools had doubled by the time of writing this book. This sees school-based enquiry now viewed in a different role in the production and consumption of evidence (see Chapter 7) and a politicisation of the term evidence-based practice (see Afterword and Clegg, 2005).

The role of digital developments for teacher networking

Teacher connectivity, whether in teams, in communities or as part of wider networks, can include face-to-face and virtual (online) interactions, so affecting teacher collaboration and engagement in enquiry. Digital technologies offer new spaces to assemble, while also enhancing offline connectivity (Fox and Bird, 2017). However, the digital world has brought work and home life into closer proximity than in previous generations, affecting teachers, as others in employment (O'Hara, 2013; The Secret Teacher, 2018). On a daily basis, contemporary teachers need to decide whether to answer work emails, engage in professionally-relevant social media activity or prepare materials, usually involving digital tools, at home. This problematises personal and professional identities, which become blurred when establishing relationships and identifying with collectives (Beijaard et al, 2004; Leijen and Kullasepp, 2013). Such activity can also be an enabler. Pre-service teachers report how using social media can help them transition into teaching by reaching out to those already in the profession beyond those they have met in person (Kontopoulou, 2019; Fox and Bird, 2017). Similarly, prior to and once in the profession, the internet gives access to a multitude of specialist forums and user groups which allow teachers to belong to new collectives than would otherwise have been possible in person. However, unresolved tensions around peer pressure, privacy, accountability to professional codes of conduct and a range of motivations to connect through social media have been evidenced (Owen et al, 2016; Fox and Bird, 2017). Further discussion about the role of social media for engaging with research is covered in Chapter 7.

2.8 Which alternative notions of collectives are useful to thinking about teacher collaboration and enquiry?

In addition to teams, communities and networks, two further collectives, neither exclusive to teachers, can help explain beyond-school interactions related to collaborating or engaging in enquiry: sets and partnerships.

What is a set and why is it helpful in thinking about teacher collaboration and enquiry?

'Sets' refer to loose aggregations of people who share a common interest: the topic and theme of interest binding people together (Dron and Anderson, 2014a). This is useful for thinking about when:

we do not know people in any meaningful way, so 'network' is too strong a word for our engagement, and sometimes we are not members of shared groups, yet people can make a big difference to our learning.

(Dron and Anderson, 2014a, p165)

In sets, sustained interactions are not needed, nor any commitment to membership or shared goal. This is useful when understanding social media activity such as joining Facebook groups, liking Facebook pages, subscribing to YouTube channels, using hashtags on Twitter or Pinterest and engaging with Wikipedia, without personally knowing the others involved in those tools. Sets enable both 'just-in-time' learning (for getting a timely answer to a specific query) and lifelong learning, by providing opportunities to keep up-to-date in a topic or interest. For example, a special education teacher interested in educating those with Down's syndrome might decide to engage through social media with a set of professionals specialising in the topic and sign up for notifications, follow particular individuals' accounts or join forums such that, through new posts/tweets, they are kept updated. Online forums, themed chats, are now an established feature of social media activity for a wide range of interests and roles, which are increasingly being studied as to their efficacy and challenges (eg Britt and Paulus, 2016; Herbert, 2012; Jefferis and Bisschoff, 2017; Robson, 2016).

What is a partnership and why is it helpful in thinking about professional learning?

According to the Collins English Dictionary (2018) '... *a partnership is a relationship in which two or more people, organizations, or countries work together as partners'* and is synonymous with co-operation, alliance and sharing. In terms of partnerships which involve teachers, there are two relevant forms: home–school and school–university partnerships. The first are between teachers and the parents/carers of those students for whom they are jointly responsible, given that teachers act in loco parentis while students are in school. Home–school agreements were statutory for schools in England and Wales from 1999 to 2016 and whole-school policies, to which parents and teachers are expected to commit, are still encouraged (Whittaker, 2016). Such mutual arrangements, although not yet universally embraced internationally (de Carvalho, 2000), have grown to replace a more transmissive model in which schools passed information to parents (Swap, 1993). Closer home–school communications can help teachers learn for example about children's motivations, personal circumstances, cultural backgrounds and level of support (eg LaRocque et al, 2011; Katyal and Evers, 2014) as well as challenging a school to examine its aspirations to inclusivity (eg Crozier and Davies, 2013; Gaitan, 2004).

These studies about the value of such partnerships are increasingly being produced in collaboration through participatory research designs involving researchers, teachers and other members of the multi-agency relationships within which schools now work. Much of this is being driven by schools' engagement in a second form of partnership: a school–university partnership. These are explored in depth in Chapter 3.

2.9 Summary

There is a rich lexicon of language associated with collaborative teacher enquiry which, once defined and differentiated, can offer insights for educational leaders to think strategically. There are benefits and challenges of teachers working in what can be conceptualised as teams, partnerships, communities and networks. This provides a context for the more detailed examination of these notions in the remainder of the book.

Table 2b

Key action	Why is this important? What is important?
Draw your personal network and identify your sources of support.	Recognise those who are already important as well as identify opportunities to strengthen or make new links.
Run an activity in which a group of colleagues draw their personal (and professional) networks to discuss where sources of support lie and how you can support one another.	Guide a discussion about developing relational capacity to support teacher collaboration and enquiry.
Identify teams within which you work. Consider how inward or outward looking the team is. Identify where external input could be drawn upon (eg from team members' personal networks) or particular expertise or experience sourced.	Avoid the danger of 'group think' through lack of external stimulation, especially if the team were self-forming. Ensure challenge and new insights are available to support teams in accomplishing tasks.

Key action	Why is this important? What is important?
Building on your responses to questions at the end of Chapter 1 undertake a Strengths–Weaknesses–Opportunities–Threats (SWOT) analysis as the basis for planning a strategy for building teacher collaboration through enquiry.	Taking stock of how your school is already operating and identifying external and internal factors will provide a sound basis for anticipating concerns and challenges, as well as where this work might align well with existing resources and agendas.

Exploring further

For a fuller overview of conceptualisations of school culture and its associated challenges than has been possible in this chapter, a synthesis by Stoll is recommended. Although not a recent publication, this pulls together key models and frameworks for thinking about culture which stand the test of time.

Stoll, L (1998) *School Culture*, reprinted from *School Improvement Network's Bulletin 9*. London: Institute of Education. [online] Available at: www. researchgate.net/publication/242721155_School_culture (accessed 25 August 2019).

For a critical overview of practical approaches to Joint Practice Development (JPD), a term which covers much of the same territory as the collaborative teacher groups outlined in this chapter, the following linked publications are recommended.

Sebba, J, Kent, P and Tregenza, J (2012) *Joint Practice Development: What Does the Evidence Suggest Are Effective Approaches?* Nottingham: National College for School Leadership. [online] Available at: https://assets.publishing.service. gov.uk/government/uploads/system/uploads/attachment_data/file/335729/jpd-what-does-the-evidence-suggest-are-effective-approaches-long.pdf (accessed 25 August 2019).

Stoll, L, Harris, A and Handscomb, G (2012) *Great Professional Development which Leads to Great Pedagogy: Nine Claims from Research Schools and Academies*. Nottingham: National College for School Leadership. [online] Available at: https://assets.publishing.service.gov.uk/government/uploads/ system/uploads/attachment_data/file/335707/Great-professional-development-which-leads-to-great-pedagogy-nine-claims-from-research.pdf (accessed 25 August 2019).

Chapter 3
School–university partnerships: contexts for enquiry

Val Poultney

3.1 Chapter overview

This chapter will outline:

3.2 the nature of school–university partnerships;

3.3 what the evidence says about school–university partnerships;

3.4 the challenges and opportunities of school–university partnerships;

3.5 case studies of partnership-working.

3.2 The nature of school–university partnerships

School–college or school–university-partnership working is not a new idea in the field of education. Training schools and colleges (also called 'normal schools') were set up by charities in the early nineteenth century to train teachers in elementary schools, with universities becoming involved in teacher training in 1890 and the establishment of 'day training colleges' (National Archives, nd). Such partnerships now play a role in most of the existing routes into teaching and this chapter focuses on how schools and universities can work together. The focus is on teacher education and in-service continuous professional development (CPD), specifically for, research/enquiry-based support. Stenhouse's Humanities Curriculum Project (Stenhouse, 1968) aimed to move teachers' then model of 'transmission teaching' to one of facilitating learning: asking open questions of their students, encouraging teachers to hypothesise. In the 1960s and 1970s the school-based curriculum reform, with significant input from projects funded by the Ford Foundation (Stenhouse, 1975), encouraged teachers to move away from teaching and testing 'facts' to a general pedagogy of 'enquiry/discovery learning' (Bruner, 1961, cited in Elliott, 2015). This encouraged teachers to consider learning opportunities through independent or self-directed thinking by their students. These ideas of 'theorising pedagogy', or 'practical theorising' (Hagger and McIntyre, 2006), provide opportunities for teachers to engage in action research to collect evidence in support of their practice. In 1970 the Centre for Applied Research in Education (CARE) was founded at the University of East Anglia in the UK, leading the *'teacher-as-researcher'* movement by supporting collaborative applied research and the integration of theory and practice. By the 1990s Goodlad (1994) proposed that schools and universities work together as *'Centres of Pedagogy'*.

The pressure to spend money wisely on teacher professional development has never been so important since the unchaining of schools from local authority control, the devolvement of budgets to schools and subsequent increased tightening of school budgets (Greany and Brown, 2015; House of Commons, 2019). Working in partnership requires partners to consider factors such as the aims and desired outcomes of the collaboration, how long it will exist and the roles and responsibilities of those involved. This includes marrying the work in the collaboration with that needed to meet partners own agendas and recognising their own accountabilities.

There is no UK government policy for how such partnerships might work but there is an unwritten expectation that schools and universities need to be reactive to the ever-changing education landscape. Although Michael Gove (2013) made clear that it was not the role of government to *'tell teachers how to teach'*, this is set against strong guidance to teachers about *'what works'* (Hattie, 2008, 2012). Much of the supporting infrastructure put in place by the UK Labour government (1997–2010) has been dismantled or slimmed down (Greany and Brown, 2015) as exemplified by the new national curriculum in 2014, the removal of the prescriptive requirement for headteachers to hold a National Professional Qualification for Headship and the merger of the National College for School Leadership, first with the Teaching Agency in 2013 to form the National College for Teaching and Leadership and, in 2018, more fundamentally, with the Department for Education. The rhetoric of the subsequent UK Conservative government policy has been to advocate a school-led improvement model, for both teacher education and continuing professional development. To accompany this, schools are needing to adjust to new accountabilities such as a new Ofsted framework (Spielman, 2019), the Early Careers Framework (DfE, 2019) and Teacher Standards for Professional Development (DfE, 2016b). As teacher education is now becoming more school-led and school-based, universities are having to re-visit their cultural values and review how their often restrictive structures can be widened so that they are better placed to engage with interdisciplinary work (Handscomb et al, 2014). As schools have been encouraged to form networks with each other and to lead on teacher education programmes such as School Direct, universities have moved to a more peripheral role, described to be more akin to *'service agents'* (Day, 2017) than the knowledge partners envisioned by Goodlad (1994).

This chapter examines how schools and universities can work together in a model of partnership that challenges teachers and school leaders to think more critically about their practice.

Types of partnership

Three forms of partnership are most commonly documented between schools and universities (based on McLaughlin and Black-Hawkins, 2007).

- **Service**: the university provides research training or some form of support for staff working in schools.

- **Complementary**: the university conducts university-initiated research in a school and supports school-initiated research.

- **Collaborative**: there is a common research or enquiry focus where research methodologies are negotiated and agreed.

In the case of the first form, both institutions play to their respective strengths and traditional roles. In the second, there is mutual engagement but limited impact on each other's agendas and in the third example there is often a great deal of adaptation on behalf of both parties. Since the 1990s the most powerful publications on school–university partnerships have been those which have been co-authored by members representing the various partners (eg Johnston and The Educators for Collaborative Change, 1997; Hargreaves, D, 1999; McLaughlin et al, 2007; Beckett, 2016; Frost, 2014, 2017; Breault, 2013). These have allowed honest accounts of the challenges as well as benefits of engaging in such boundary-crossing collaborations. Case studies in this chapter illustrate such collaborative partnership approaches.

3.3 What the evidence says about school–university partnerships

Devolvement of budgets to schools and a focus on school-led models of teacher development have arguably made professional development more insular and open to poor practice (Handscomb et al, 2014). Teachers are, however, not unaccustomed to working as part of PLCs (Day, 2017; Stoll et al, 2018) either within their own schools or externally with other teachers. A study commissioned to examine the transfer of *'good practice'* (Fielding et al, 2005) concluded that JPD was the way forward, arguing that traditional methods of professional development (bespoke events sharing good or best practice) had limited value. The same conclusions were drawn five years later in the State of the Nation review of CPD in England (Opfer and Pedder, 2011b). Successful JPD is characterised by having robust leadership, establishment of networks, working in a culture of trust and supported work with partners (Sebba et al, 2012). Similarly, effective PLCs have been concluded to need strong school leadership which includes work in external partnerships (Handscomb et al, 2014). Yet McLaughlin and Black-Hawkins (2007) found that practitioners who engaged in research and enquiry tended to do so individually in their own classrooms, linked to their own professional interests. Even when departmental or whole school enquiry was engaged, while valuable, the knowledge generated for teaching often remained localised within a school due to the prevalence of siloed ways of working. There is a potential, however, as exemplified in a case study later in this chapter, for school–university partnerships utilising JPD to extend opportunities for practitioners to expand their knowledge creation through widening links with practitioners and academics and offering alternative routes for dissemination of new knowledge. This can help fulfil leadership visions to offer staff the opportunity to work in an '*expansive workplace*' (Fuller and Unwin, 2004).

3.4 The challenges and opportunities for partnership-working

This chapter now turns to some of the reported opportunities and challenges facing school–university partnerships.

Challenge: clash of cultures

It is well documented in the literature (Smedley, 2001; Taylor, 2008; Breault, 2013; Maskit and Orland-Barak, 2015) that there are significant cultural differences between schools and universities. School agendas are often political, centralised agendas where quick-fix solutions are encouraged, whereas a university is seen as a gatekeeper to wider educational knowledge. This could be interpreted as universities having a paternalistic, hierarchical and self-interested view of their role in the educational landscape (Gove, 2013), which implies a dominance of theory to have power over practice.

The professional development of teachers is by its very nature a collaborative endeavour, yet because of the structures of both schools and universities, the work of teachers and academics is largely individual. As already discussed in Chapter 2, there may be relatively few opportunities for teachers to work together collaboratively because most of their work happens in classrooms. Similarly, for academics, lecturing, research, writing and publication are often highly individualised. As noted in Chapter 1, Teaching Schools and Alliances now have responsibility for implementing continuing professional development and R&D (Husbands, 2015). This change in policy continues to challenge universities and schools to reconsider how they might now work together in support of this remit, bringing opportunities and risks for both partners. Before partnerships are established, a careful and critical self-evaluation is needed to recognise assumptions held. For example, to identify where there is a perceived danger for one side to hold power over the other, or where there are insufficient resources significant consultation, negotiation and problem-solving.

Opportunity: working towards democratic learning

Structures need to be sufficiently flexible to allow all participants to take part in key decision-making, such that a trusting working relationship can grow (Bain et al, 2017). One such approach is the use of appreciative enquiry. In this *dialogues about teaching and learning are perceived to be appreciated rather than threatening to professional identity* and through which *problems of practice* become *challenges of expanding practice* (Day, 2017, p 129). Any perceived differences between academics and teachers in status, agendas and power differentials need to be overcome as a form of social reform (Zeichner, 2010) towards establishing governance of and for the partnership. Again, dialogue is needed to demonstrate a commitment to equity. Such social negotiation, involving give and take among partners, is the bedrock of democratic learning (Johnston and the Educators for Collaborative Change, 1997) and the foundation of trusting reciprocal partnerships (Poultney and Fordham, 2017; Philpott and Poultney, 2018). Taylor (2008) regards partnership as a vehicle where learning is placed centrally to everyone.

Challenge: teachers looking for quick fixes

The work of teachers and of academics is inherently different and bound by time and context. Zeichner (2010) sees this as a problem of *disconnect* between the two institutions. The context in which teachers and academics learn is different. Teachers are likely to focus on children's learning, learning about teaching and learning about oneself in a professional development context. Academics learn how to: theorise practice, present their work academically in line with their academic community and think about oneself as a teacher educator. In terms of supply and demand, the busyness of teachers' lives demands quick fixes to inform classroom decision-making and a receptiveness for *what works* evidence (Hattie, 2008, 2012; Slavin, 2004). While education research is also designed to understand and support teachers' work and hence children's learning, research work is a time-consuming endeavour. Academics need time to examine the link between theory and practice and do so across many authors' work (eg Yamagata-Lynch and Smaldino, 2007). While the outcomes of research are likely to be relevant to schools these are not easy to either access or implement in their settings, as discussed further in Chapter 7.

Opportunity: working democratically to expand knowledge bases

Partnerships allow school and university educators to engage jointly in research and rethinking of practice, thus creating an opportunity for the profession to expand its knowledge base by *'putting research into practice and practice into research'* (Handscomb et al, 2014; Snow and Marshall, 2010, p 482; Waterhouse et al, 2013). Evidence-based teaching and teacher enquiry in school–university partnerships, in which neither academics nor teachers dominate and both parties are committed to finding ways of learning democratically together (Beckett, 2016), are likely to be transformative (Poultney and Fordham, 2017, 2018). To build intellectual capital across a partnership, commitment to dissemination is also needed. This is likely to involve a combination of events (eg meetings, seminars, workshops and conferences) hosted by either partner, including informal networking spaces or *'muffin chats'* (Watson and Drew, 2017), and publications (eg blogs, newsletters, joint research papers or a book).

Challenge: building capacity and agency for change

There will be a transaction cost for everyone in terms of investing time, energy and sustained commitment to the partnership (Handscomb et al, 2014). University organisational structures may restrict interdisciplinary working and commitment to partnership-working. On both sides, budgetary constraints are also likely to challenge the capacity for partnership-working. As noted earlier, there are likely to be challenges associated with the directionality of the partnership, if teachers perceive that their practice knowledge is being treated as inferior to academic theory (Lynch and Smith, 2004) or that they do not see the value of academic knowledge, if it is perceived as not directly implementable to their work. Such factors will affect teachers' intrinsic motivation to engage.

Partnerships are therefore inherently risky ventures, often uncertain and with potential to fail. Changes to government policy or institutional re-organisations can also threaten the existence of a partnership. Change agendas as a result of the work of the partnership may be harder to implement and everyone would need to be clear on how the outcomes will be implemented.

Opportunity: creating the third space for partnership-working

The intersectionality between the school and the university creates a *'third space'* in which professional development discourse can be encouraged and facilitated (Broadhead, 2010; Handscomb et al, 2014; Greany and Brown, 2015). This requires a new form of partnership governance to be established, which can strategically and structurally support creative working in a culture of trust, mutuality and respect (Hargreaves and Fullan, 2012). A culture is needed to deal with the likely tensions arising from differences in opinion and partners not knowing how their ideas might be received in spaces of dialogue. Learning opportunities can then arise from the chance to share and appreciate differences of opinion drawing from a broader collective experience than would be the case within either of the partner organisations.

If teachers are to be both consumers and producers of research then they need to be able to interrogate their practice (British Educational Research Association (BERA–RSA), 2014). The *'third space'* is an opportunity to work collaboratively, in a growth-promoting, learning-orientated way, where sharing ideas through critical discourse can support teachers in this interrogation (Watson, 2014; Dunn et al, 2017). In terms of time and money and in an ever-changing educational landscape, the nature of these spaces needs to be under regular review. As discussed in Chapter 7 there is the potential for technology to play a role in partnership-working.

Challenge: leadership matters

As part of the development of governance of partnerships, leadership from both partners needs to elide. Organisational leaders need to have a good understanding of partnership work so that they can evaluate the opportunities and challenges that it might bring to their organisation. Partnership-working can exist without senior leadership support but will have limitations. One consideration is how outcomes might politically affect a leader's own leadership position. Another is to recognise the differences in thinking between teachers and academics, which might cause tensions for leaders (Fordham, 2017). It is also important to be alert to how relationships can change over time. Proactivity will be needed to work towards developing and sustaining shifts in power relationships as the partnership moves towards an equitable relationship. The notions of teacher leadership, discussed at various points in this book (Frost, 2014, 2017; Katyal and Evers, 2014; Lieberman and Miller, 2001; Stoll et al, 2018) are a way for thinking about this across schools and their partnerships.

Opportunity: working as 'boundary spanners' or 'blended professionals'

Working across institutional boundaries is a role for those who lead on partnerships – as *'boundary spanners'* (Tsui and Law, 2007) or *'blended professionals'* (Handscomb et al, 2014). As noted above, both school-based and university-based leadership is needed. Agreeing on a focus for the work, recognising strengths and experience of others and how and when to communicate are all important shared considerations. This will help to build social capital (Putnam, 1995) by broadening networks which bridge across shared interests of both school and academic communities, generating joint knowledge for the benefit of both communities and ultimately building trust between partners.

3.5 Case studies

The first case study does not present a typical school–university partnership but considers how important it is to maintain strong leadership from both school and university perspectives. Without this most partnerships will fail. The second case study is an anonymised account of the opportunities and challenges based on the authors' experiences as part of partnership work in a Teaching School Alliance.

Case study 1

Reciprocal leadership

A primary school that was under Ofsted-imposed Special Measures began work with a local university academic in order to encourage teachers and school leaders to engage with evidence-based teaching methods. The headteacher wanted to critically evaluate the impact of various initiatives beyond the gathering of school data as progress indicators. After working together for two years and seeing positive outcomes for the school (now graded 'Good'), the university academic was looking for a means to research/evaluate the merit of their partnership-working. The headteacher and academic saw themselves as leaders in their respective institutions and therefore any evaluation of their work would involve them as both participants and informants of that work.

The academic was interested in the characteristics and competencies both needed in order to make their partnership work, and be sustained. They generated three research questions.

1. What does our leadership relationship look like and how do we conceptualise it?

2. What are the conditions, processes and actions for us to consider as we establish our partnership?

3. How might we gather evidence of our partnership relationship and how might we go about this?

Both agreed that they were working in a relational paradigm where power was shared and that they worked democratically to make progress on their collective vision for the school. When undertaking a literature review, using key words such as 'reciprocal leadership' and 'authentic leadership', the academic came across an inventory named 'Conscious Quotient inventory' (CQ-i) developed by a Romanian professor of psychology, Ovidiu Brazdau (2016). This had been used to investigate the characteristics of participative leadership in a university context. It explores aspects of what it is to be human in all its forms and both academic and headteacher thought this to be a good starting point to take the 'temperature' of their partnership.

The inventory covers seven domains of consciousness:

1. physical CQ (being conscious of your own body and environmental awareness);

2. emotional CQ (conscious of your own feelings, emotions, their development and interactions);

3. cognitive CQ (conscious of your ideas, thoughts, reflective processes, meaning-making);

4. social-relational CQ (conscious of human relationships and the way you connect with others);

5. self CQ (conscious of self and one's own ego or identity);

6. inner growth CQ (capacity for awareness of personal development, personal growth);

7. spiritual CQ (conscious of yourself as part of a wider world and your place/connections in it, 'I' as an observer).

Both partners completed the audit and reconvened to discuss results. They felt the merit of the inventory lay in focusing on their own awareness of self and how they related to others, in ways which they imagined could have value to others in leadership positions. They used the outcomes (scores) to guide their discussions on how the partnership arrangement had been successful and why. They concluded that the inventory benchmarked their ways of partnership-working through a reflective approach, which enabled both partners to better understand each other's respective roles and obligations in their school and university setting. Although the scores were designed to be personal, and not to be shared, these partners felt that sharing scores allowed them to review the partnership as a social activity from which both benefitted. To allow for this shared learning experience it needed to be conducted at a time when there was sufficient trust. This allowed the inventory to support sociocratic ways of working and provided quantifiable measures of each other's personal dispositions in a professional context. By putting this partnership under the microscope, critical dialogue was generated around such areas as spirituality, which might never have been had without completing the CQ-i. (Poultney and Fordham, 2018).

JPD as focus for partnership work

In a different English context, a Teaching School Alliance, as part of their R&D work, secured funding through two national projects to support collaborative teacher enquiry through Lesson Study. The Alliance was partnered with three universities who took an active role on the R&D committee to support the school in its research work. Through this work academics advised on many elements of research through workshops and conferences including approaches to research, classroom observation protocols and the ethics of researching in classroom/school contexts. This engagement with teachers both at a strategic (Alliance R&D committee) level and at a school (classroom) level helped to encourage departmental staff to see the opportunities afforded by partnership-working where academics could advise on research and be on hand to help with data analysis.

In self-evaluatory research undertaken by the Alliance about these teachers' experience of engaging with Lesson Study, JPD was concluded to provide an environment where individual teacher professional identity, professional capacity and agency were enhanced, with teachers developing real passion for enquiry work as part of their practice. Lesson Study helped teachers to have a positive impact on student learning and on their own professional learning and helped reaffirm their commitment to teaching and the profession more widely.

This evaluation also revealed limitations in a school's leadership to provide effective structure, support and resources for teacher research. Despite a lack of explicit and sustained leadership support, subject leads continued with Lesson Study as they could see the value of JPD as having a positive impact on student learning. Academic partners agreed with teachers but observed that, from a quality assurance perspective, school leaders, Teaching Schools and their Alliances all need to be accountable for partnership enquiry. This needs to be at both strategic and school level, especially where projects have been funded. Having better formal agreements from the very start would have enabled these projects' outcomes to be disseminated more widely to contribute to school improvement across the school and the Alliance to avoid entrenching siloed ways of working.

3.6 Summary

School–university partnerships bring together theory and practice and can keep practitioners and education academics connected in a changing education landscape. However, partnership-working is inherently a challenging business as there are differences to be accepted and potential tensions to be resolved. That is why, for a partnership to be successful, it is crucial to have support from institutional leaders, robust planning and the energy to see the project through to completion. While changes in internal or external context are inevitable, through negotiation and dialogue, partnership-working can open opportunities for everyone to learn, create new knowledge and solve problems of practice. This generation of intellectual capital builds the credibility of all participants and can contribute, through appropriate dissemination, to school improvement at a local, regional and possibly wider level.

Questions for partnership-working

Planning is an essential feature of partnership-working. The following table offers a checklist of some of the important considerations that partners should have under review during this planning phase. The list is not exhaustive – different partnerships will experience different challenges and opportunities. Create a third column and populate with your responses in terms of actions relevant to your setting. This will enable you to see where further information is required before embarking on partnership-working.

Table 3a Key questions when planning to enter into a partnership

Key questions	Why they are important? What is important about them?
What is the aim of the partnership and what is to be achieved by it?	Partnership-working requires a focus (aim) and objectives for how the work is to be carried out. A specific outcome for the project will help keep everyone focused.
Who is involved?	This type of work can be done with two or many partners, but it is important they are identified from the beginning.
What is the time frame for this partnership?	Funding may dictate how long the project will run for but agreements over start and finish dates are vital for everyone involved.
Who is leading on the venture and are they known to all participants?	An identified leader or leaders are vital to keep the team on track and focused on the work. These roles need to be clearly identified and agreed by all.

Key questions	Why they are important? What is important about them?
What resources are currently available and what resources do you need to procure?	All resources need to be carefully considered and planned for so that the project can achieve its aims.
Who is planning the project and for how long will it be run?	This is best identified at the beginning of the project and clearly set out in formal agreements.
Who are the colleagues that need to work with you to realise your goal?	Some colleagues may be on the team for the life of the project and others at certain stages so, in planning for this, colleagues need to be identified and sourced.
Are there any formalities you need to establish for when the partnership is in operation, such as agreement from respective leadership teams?	School and university protocols will be different so both parties need to identify any restrictions from either institution before the start of the project. This will probably happen in the planning phase.
Will a formal partnership agreement be put in place?	This may be in the form of a contract between institutions, identifying roles and responsibilities for staff and matters related to funding, administration, life of the project, ownership and use of intellectual property.
What administrative tasks need to be achieved to support the partnership including budgeting?	If external funding has been secured, knowledge of how the budget will operate over the life of the project and how the money can be spent is needed.
How will the intellectual knowledge generated by the partnership be reported upon by (a) the school and (b) the university?	Intellectual capital generated as a result of the project will benefit from dissemination to wider audiences but there needs to be agreement between institutions as to the ownership and use of intellectual property.

Key questions	Why they are important? What is important about them?
How will communications be facilitated between partners?	Everyone needs to be clear on these and when to be involved to achieve parity of working practices.
How will partnership work be sustained if changes to staffing occur?	This can never be fully planned for but is an important consideration if there is a will or onus to complete the project.
What quality assurance (QA) measures are in place for the partnership?	It is important to carry out regular monitoring of the partnership by designated person/s who would monitor and evaluate outcomes on a regular basis. Where possible a third (external) party might be employed to carry out an impartial evaluation of the partnership especially around 'value for money' issues and long-term partnerships.
How can the outcomes of partnership work be disseminated more widely?	Dissemination of new knowledge is a vital part of partnership-working to reach new audiences, both professional and academic. It is important to agree how this intellectual capital will be used in the school and university setting. For example, routes to publishing can be supported by university academics. This work builds credibility for teachers and academics and contributes to locally produced evidence that sustains school improvement with opportunities to share more widely.

Exploring further

Greany, T and Brown, C (2015) Partnerships Between Teaching Schools and Universities. London Centre for Leadership in Learning, UCL Institute of Education. [online] Available at: www.researchlearningcommunities.org/uploads/2/1/6/3/21631832/_teaching_schools_and_universities_research_report.pdf (accessed 2 October 2019).

Handscomb, G, Gu, Q and Varley, M (2014) School–University Partnerships: Fulfilling the Potential. Literature Review. National Co-ordinating Centre for Public Engagement. [online] Available at: www.publicengagement.ac.uk/sites/default/files/publication/supi_project_report_final.pdf (last accessed 26 August 2019).

Townsend, A (2019) Situating Partnership Activity, An Activity Theory Inspired Analysis of School to School Inquiry Networks. *Cogent Education*. [online] Available at: https://doi.org/10.1080/2331186X.2019.1576424 (accessed 1 October 2019).

Useful websites

To find out more about the work of the Centre for Applied Research in Education go to: www.uea.ac.uk/education/research/care

The Conscious Quotient inventory can be accessed at: www.consciousness-quotient.com where there is more information about how to use it. Please note it was designed to be used individually and there are ethical considerations to consider should you choose to share your information with others, or they with you.

Chapter 4
Teacher-led enquiry

Alison Fox

4.1 Chapter overview

This chapter will outline:

4.2   a history of the development of ideas and practices about teacher-led enquiry;

4.3   challenges associated with teacher-led enquiry;

4.4   features of different forms of teacher-led enquiry;

4.5   case studies of collaborative teacher-led enquiry.

This chapter builds on discussions in Chapters 2 and 3 about how UK schools and the teachers who make up the professional workforce are responding to changing expectations of them to increasingly provide school-based evidence for the development of practice. While born from ideas of teachers as important producers of research, an identity which has been advocated since the 1960s (see section 2.3), it can be questioned whether there is currently a political appetite, at least in the UK, for teachers' contribution to be seen in this light.

Different options for teacher-led enquiry are presented including those already covered such as JPD (Stoll et al, 2012a), reflections on the significance of practitioner action research as part of formal study (ITE, master's and professional doctorate) and the role of informal school-based enquiry (eg McNiff, 2010). It should be noted that throughout this chapter, wherever teachers are named as associated with enquiry, this also includes other practitioners including teaching and classroom assistants and training teachers.

4.2 A brief history of teacher-led enquiry

Teachers' involvement in the production of evidence can be traced back to the work of the Carnegie Foundation for the Advancement of Teaching in 1905 which was set up by a United States of America Act of Congress as a Policy and Research Centre called to *'do and perform all things necessary to encourage, uphold, and dignify the profession of the teacher and the cause of higher education'* (Carnegie Foundation, 2019; Park and Takahashi, 2013). National work in support of developing teaching as a profession took place in the United States and across Europe with, by the 1960s, teachers becoming recognised as autonomous professionals and being offered opportunities to engage with school-based curriculum development projects (Hargreaves, A, 2000). By the 1970s initiatives proliferated (Hargreaves, A, 1982) as external contexts increasingly began to affect what happened in schools. The work of teachers and teachers working in isolated ways became recognised as unproductive (Little, 1990; Hargreaves, A, 2000). As introduced in Chapters 2 and 3, collective approaches to growing the profession can be traced to the *'teacher-as-researcher'* movement (Stenhouse, 1975). Despite the UEA CARE Centre led by John Elliott closing in 2015, the Classroom Action Research Network (1976), later renamed the Collaborative Action Research Network (University of East Anglia, 2019; Somekh, 2010), is still active, it supports and connects teachers engaging in research personally, locally, nationally and internationally and publishing an academic journal *Educational Action Research* (Collaborative Action Research Network-Action Learning: Action Research Association, CARN-ALARA, 2019).

During the last 50 years some noteworthy initiatives have been seminal in valuing and driving school-led enquiry. Notions of schools as learning organisations (Senge, 1990) in which there is a central role for teacher enquiry gained international traction during the 1980s and 1990s as an ideal for school reform (eg DuFour, 1997; O'Neil, 1995). However, it was critiqued for its ability to be realised in practice (eg Fullan, 1995). As noted in Chapter 2 the 1990s saw advocation of enquiry-based *'teacher leadership'* (Lieberman and Miller, 2001) in the United States of America, including the National Writing Project (Lieberman and Wood, 2002) and the Carnegie Academy for the Scholarship of Teaching and Learning, running programmes since 2007 (Illinois State University, 2019). The increasingly collaborative and inter-organisational benefits of teacher-led enquiry led to discussions in the UK about the power of networking (as introduced in Chapter 2), with the instigation of nationally funded waves of schools (2002–2006) sharing the work and learning from their enquiries as part of NLCs (eg Jackson and Temperley, 2006). However, how substantively enquiry has been embedded in any of these initiatives has been challenged. Enquiry, while found to be highly valued by teachers as part of their development and professional learning (Pedder, 2006), was found to be lacking in the State of the Nation review of CPD provision and access commissioned by the Training and Development Agency in England (Opfer and Pedder, 2011a).

In the 2010s and moving into the 2020s, as discussed further in Chapter 7, greater emphasis is being given, in the UK at least, on teachers being seen principally as consumers of research, reviewing published evidence about *'what works'* (EEF, 2019; Hattie, 2008, 2012; Higgins et al, 2014; Sutton Trust, 2012–2018; Waak, 2019). This chapter offers a critical and broad view of the landscape of contemporary teacher-led enquiry.

In 2003 Judyth Sachs wrote a book called *The Activist Teaching Profession* (Sachs, 2003) voicing her concerns about how teachers were viewed, at a time when teacher accountability and performance had come to the fore through standardised tests and the initiation of school and system ranking. This was written as a call to action, Sachs saw the profession as needing to enhance its status, calling teachers to reclaim their agency and professionalism by being more transparent about their practices in classrooms and hence rebuild trust with both those in political power and local communities. Over ten years later, Sachs reanalysed the status of the profession (Sachs, 2016). She acknowledged that a performance culture was now deeply embedded and accountability measures, such as targets and standards, had become the tools for managing and overseeing teacher work. As noted in Chapter 2, RCTs had become the gold standard mechanism to generate evidence, aimed at informing the teaching profession about which interventions 'work' and, hence, how teachers should practice. According to Sachs, the result is a more conservative and risk-averse teaching profession, or *'controlled or compliant professionalism'* (Sachs, 2016, p 423). The danger, already anticipated by Cochran-Smith and Lytle (2009), was that, with a focus on the means and not ends of education, teachers now face a re-emergence of a transmission model for teaching and learning. This is accompanied by an exclusion of teachers as valued knowledge-producers and innovators accompanied by a lack of investment in them as producers and co-producers of new knowledge needed for the future of the profession. As noted in Chapter 3 this limits the profession to dealing with the problems of the present with quick-fix solutions. Further, teachers become '*silent witnesses*' to the demise of their profession (Sachs, 2016, p 424). Sachs's contemporary call to action is for the profession to create spaces for further collaboration and to become engaged with enquiry for ongoing professional growth. This chapter charts how a practitioner research movement is, despite this constraining educational policy and political climate, thriving worldwide.

4.3 Challenges associated with teacher-led enquiry

> Isn't teacher enquiry just reflective practice, with which we expect all teachers to be involved as part of being a professional and developing practice?
>
> (Cain, 2017; Postholm, 2009)

> Enquiry, particularly collaborative enquiry, involves time over and above an already full schedule of activity focused on planning and delivering learning opportunities for students and monitoring and assessing their progress.
>
> (Cain, 2017; Thompson and Thompson, 2008)

> Enquiry is not valued by senior leaders in our setting. If we want to be released to observe one another teach or to organise a meeting to plan and discuss enquiry, there is no space in the timetable and no support for covering our teaching or missing meetings.
>
> (Thompson and Thompson, 2008)

> We don't feel we have the right skills to carry out effective enquiry and yet there is no support for us accessing training which would help develop our skills. We need to self-fund master's study and the school does not have strong links with universities who might be able to support us in research skill development.
>
> (Borg, and Sanchez, 2015; DeLuca et al, 2017)

4.4 Features of different forms of teacher-led enquiry

Before distinguishing between different forms of teacher-led enquiry, it is worth distinguishing between practitioner research and reflective practice. There is a tradition of teachers being trained to be reflective on, about and for their practice so as to adjust how they teach. Teachers make their decisions depending on the group of young people in front of them and their knowledge about pupils understanding and prior experiences. This was encapsulated as Donald Schön's and his notion of the *'reflective practitioner'* (Schön, 1984). By defining research as *'systematic enquiry made public'* (Stenhouse, 1975, p 142) Stenhouse challenged teachers to extend their reflective practice into practitioner research. Therefore, enquiry is the systematic gathering of evidence, by which there is clear link between the enquiry questions, the research design and the methods used to collect evidence. It is also expected that the findings of enquiry not only inform the practitioner's practice but are also disseminated further to other audiences. That teachers are involved in, and ideally drive, enquiry offers an approach to the development of teaching practices (whether related to curriculum, pedagogy and/or assessment) which does not rely on external bodies specifying new practices for teachers to implement.

A typology of teacher-led enquiry

To reflect on the landscape of teacher-led enquiry, four general types of enquiry are covered, recognising their scale (whether undertaken alone or with others) and formality (Table 4a). These types are discussed in relation to the challenges and opportunities they afford teachers.

Table 4a A typology of teacher-led enquiry

	Collaborative	Individual
Informal	Collaborative action-research Lesson Study Learning Rounds	Any 'systematic enquiry made public' Action research
Formal	Funded joint professional development including Lesson Study	Initial teacher education, masters or doctoral enquiry

Individual, informal enquiry

There are teachers whose reflective practice is structured and who disseminate their findings to colleagues, which could be considered a form of individual, informal enquiry. The vision and skills for such practice are likely to result from some form of research training, whether during a first degree, from continuing professional development, for example from mentor training, or from post-graduate study. Teachers can be proactive in using their time to enquire about their practice, if they are confident in understanding the research process – from setting research questions through design to collecting data, analysis and generation of findings. A challenge to those wanting to be involved in enquiry is to carve time in already busy workloads. Even for those intrinsically motivated, proactive teachers who prioritise such enquiry, a supportive school leadership is needed (Fordham, 2017). School leaders are needed to provide permission for teachers to collect data which is to be shared. How this is managed with learners and their guardians is an aspect of enquiry which needs ethical considerations to be thought through and enacted. Practitioner research undertaken informally by teachers often takes the form of action research, a cyclical form of research which involves planning, acting, reflection and evaluation leading to amendments in practice. There are many accessible texts for teachers to guide enacting action research (eg Anderson et al, 2007; McNiff and Whitehead, 2010).

Collaborative, informal enquiry

As schools take on medical-inspired practices such as learning rounds/walks (Philpott and Poultney, 2018), these can also provide teachers with evidence to inform their future practice. Action research has developed into a myriad of enquiry practices many of which are collaborative (eg CARN-ALARA, 2019; Elliott, 2015). Readers might have heard of action science, participatory action research, community-based action research, co-operative enquiry, self-study, emancipatory praxis variants (Anderson et al, 2007). Some conceptualisations prioritise the action, some the reflection and some the collaborative/community and co-operative aspects. Action research as a form of practitioner research has global reach and, as noted earlier, is the basis of the CARN network (Somekh, 2010). Although a distinctive feature of action research is that it is conducted by insider-researchers, as indicated with reference to Stenhouse (1968, 1975) and Elliott's curriculum projects (1980) in Chapter 3, this does not exclude roles for others acting as critical friends or knowledgeable others from beyond the context. This is also true of other forms of collaborative practitioner research, such as Lesson Study (see Chapter 5). Collaborative action research offers practitioners a chance to work with others to increase the potential for professional learning and to affect more students than is possible as an individual. However, even more so than for individual enquiry, these collaborative forms make further demands on time as they require teachers to find the time to meet with one another and, if engaging with those from beyond their setting – usually as part of school–university partnerships for example in Teaching School Alliances (see Chapter 3) – also to communicate with them.

Individual, formal enquiry

Individuals also undertake enquiry in ways that require standards for the enquiry to be met, as part of accredited study. This could be as part of initial teacher education-, master's- or doctoral-related enquiry. Formal study involves fees, part of which purchase for the pre-service or in-service teacher a research-methods training, access to subscription-only publications and supervision for their projects. This supports teachers in developing a research literacy and competency which not only supports them in completing valid, worthwhile and reliable studies during their accredited programme but also gives them the potential to use these skills and understandings afterwards. Research-trained practitioners can champion enquiry in their setting (Frost, 2008), share their expertise, their resources and encourage for others to engage.

Formal study is potentially available to teachers throughout their career cycle, meaning that in principle support for individual enquiry is available to all teachers. There is regular discussion in the UK about the benefits of master's study and its link to teacher professionalism, including exploring whether teaching should and could become a master's-level profession (TEAN, 2019a, 2019b). However, there are two main barriers. The key issue is sourcing funding. Self-funding has become the usual option for teachers (Arthur et al, 2006), as schools have become employers with reduced budgets for CPD and direct governmental funding is withdrawn (Zhang, 2006). A second issue linked to all enquiry, is: finding time to take on these additional activities. If accredited study is not supported with workload discussions by a practitioner's employer, it becomes particularly challenging to sustain.

Collaborative, formal enquiry

JPD, as introduced in Chapter 2, was defined by the National College as:

> **the process by which individuals, schools or other organisations learn from one another involv[ing] interaction and mutual development, sometimes co-constructing new ways of working**

(Sebba et al, 2012, p 4)

As referred to in Chapters 1 and 2, JPD was the focus of a national project involving Teacher Alliances (Stoll et al, 2012b) and included in a RCT led by CUREE (Churches, 2016), so making the Alliances externally accountable. The publications cited were authored by the evaluating universities, rather than the collaborating Teaching Alliances, as part of the funding arrangement. In turn they too needed to hold the participating schools within their Alliance to account: therefore offering a form of formality to these enquiries. Such supported studies have the potential benefits of offering financial support to release teachers' time for collective enquiry, to facilitate knowledge mobilisation and engagement with the Alliances more widely. While teachers could expect support for their research-skill development to match the expectations that their studies will be quality assured (Tregenza et al, 2012), there is international evidence that finances are not always steered by senior leaders in this way (Akiba and Wilkinson, 2016). This is in part due to the change in national funding culture towards prioritising particular forms of evidence-based practice.

Formality can also be associated with accredited studies which include collaborative enquiry, even when individuals gain individual accreditation. Collaboration might relate to those within the courses, such as initial teacher education courses using Action Research (Levin and Rock, 2003) or Lesson Study (Cajkler et al, 2013; Cajkler and Wood, 2016), school–university-partnership master's programmes (Frost, 2013; Kershner et al, 2012) and also internationally, for example the Erasmus Mundus-funded course in Special Education Needs between universities in the Netherlands, the UK and the Czech Republic (Van Swet et al, 2012).

Formal enquiry is something best supported at a national level to recognise its value. This is in place for example in educational systems such as Finland, where teaching is a master's-level profession (Kennedy, 2015), and Japan and China, where collaborative Lesson Study is an expected part of a teachers' work pattern (covered in Chapter 5).

This chapter has outlined how, despite lack of external support, teachers are engaging with meaningful enquiry and producing knowledge of, about and for practice. All four quadrants of enquiry can be evidenced, despite lack of national funding, with partners finding ways to engage with each other in its collaborative forms. Case studies are offered to illustrate school-level, regional and international teacher-led enquiry and practice development. Chapter 7 will explore the relationship between teachers and research further, focusing on them as consumers of research.

4.5 Case studies

The first case study presents enquiry in a regional Teaching School Alliance drawing on university partners which contributes to national knowledge-building and the second a regional school–university partnership network which contributes to evidence-building for practice development internationally.

Case study 1

Research and development in a Teaching School Alliance

The Royal Society for the encouragement of Arts, Manufactures and Commerce (RSA) supports a Teaching School Alliance in the West Midlands to embed teacher enquiry into its structure and activities (www.rsaacademiesteachingschool.org.uk/researchanddevelopment). The Alliance of seven schools is led by three academies designated as National Teaching Schools and hence are accountable to offering R&D, as well as school-to-school support as part of the TS 'Big 6' expectations. The Alliance offers a fellowship programme aimed at recently qualified teachers to engage in action research projects (www.rsaacademiesteachingschool.org.uk/what-we-offer/enquiry-fellowship). Teachers join the programme annually as a cohort and are supported by an external academic consultant acting as a coach. Teachers engage face-to-face in one full-day and two twilight sessions as well as having access to the coach by Skype and email to offer time and support for engagement. The Alliance reports that this balance of time offers the space and support to engage with a full cycle of action-research enquiry, while minimising the impact of the enquiry work on curriculum time. Teachers are helped in gaining access to relevant research literature to inform and locate their studies more widely, and each study is then published in the Alliance's own journal *Enquiry Fellowship*. Enquiry is also included in the programme for training teachers, who are guided to set research questions and undertake small-scale evidence collection to inform their practice. This blog post, for example, summarises the topics covered in one particular year: www.rsaacademies.org.uk/research-enquiries-rsa-teacher-trainees. The Alliance have also been working beyond their regional members and were selected by the National College in 2014–2015 to co-ordinate a project with 14 other Teaching School Alliances to develop a framework for R&D to inform what would become known as 'Research Rich' Schools. For further information about how this is envisioned and what this involves, see: www.rsaacademies.org.uk/projects/research-rich-schools

Case study 2

Teacher-led development work as a form of enquiry

HertsCam is a network which provides programmes to enable teachers to lead change in their schools, while building professional knowledge within the network. The approach is the vision of David Frost, who was an academic based at the University of Cambridge. It is founded on a programme of Teacher Led Development Work (TLDW) across schools in the county of Hertfordshire and beyond. TLDW involves practitioners in carrying out small-scale projects characterised as 'development work' (Frost et al, 2018) while being supported by membership of a group facilitated by an experienced teacher. This mentor has been inducted into the role and provided with materials and tools. Participants in TLDW are seen as leaders of change: not just changing their own practice but changing practices around them in their school, so embodying notions of teacher leadership (Frost, 2018). The key challenge is that teachers and teaching assistants often do not feel that they have the right to develop knowledge. However, the programme builds practitioner confidence, develops participants' capacity to challenge assumptions and builds empowerment. The HertsCam MEd in Leading Teaching and Learning grew out of a university-led master's programme for teachers in Hertfordshire. Increasingly, graduates of this programme took on roles as activists, supervisors and tutors. In 2014 the programme was re-designed by HertsCam and validated by the University of Hertfordshire as a course entirely led and taught by practitioners. A journal entitled *Teacher Leadership* was set up to report projects and, more recently, books have been published, with master's students and their supervisors co-authoring chapters (Frost, 2014, 2017; Frost et al, 2018). Knowledge generated by the studies does not rely on awaiting such post-study dissemination. Those involved in the TLDW and MEd programmes are expected to present narratives of their projects at regular network events hosted by different network schools, engaging attendees in discussion about the design and impact of their development work. As a result of these events, clusters of practitioners informally develop around similar topics across settings. This approach to system-wide teacher-led knowledge development has now been established in a number of settings in countries around the world. Conferences in these settings, funded by the HertsCam network and its international partners, provide still further opportunities for HertsCam practitioners to present their development work and learn about projects led by their peers in other contexts.

4.6 Summary

This chapter offers a history of initiatives which offer a rationale and support for teacher-led enquiry. Four types of enquiry in which teachers can become involved are identified: individual-informal, collaborative-informal, individual-formal and collaborative-formal. An overview of each form of enquiry has been covered, as well as identifying key barriers which limit such enquiry. In the UK at the time of publication the challenges are principally a lack of national policy or funding which advocates teachers as producers of evidence, favouring top-down and large-scale studies which teachers are encouraged to consume. However, this book series offers a contribution to remedy this situation and make the case for evidence-based practice which fundamentally includes teachers (and other related practitioners, including training teachers).

Questions for enquiry in your own school

Seven key features of collaborative teacher enquiry have been identified by the Ontario Ministry of Education (Ontario Ministry of Education, 2010). These features can be used to drive questions to inform planning, monitoring and evaluating collaborative teacher enquiry.

Feature	Key question	Key considerations
1.	Is the focus of the enquiry relevant to student learning?	Review which aspects of curriculum, pedagogy or assessment teachers and students report as challenging.
2.	Is the enquiry process a shared one among partners, involving meaningful collaboration?	If negotiation is needed, each collaborator will need a voice and the chance to align the enquiry to their agendas.
3.	Is reflection a key part of the enquiry process informing decision-making and actions?	Individual and then collective reflection require space and time in an already busy working week. This should be a safe space to ask questions and challenge assumptions about practice.
4.	Will the enquiry be iterative, such that understanding grows from cycles of enquiry?	All concerned will need to accept that enquiry of complex learning and teaching will not be a quick fix and sustainable plans for collaborative enquiry are needed.
5.	Is the enquiry based on reasoning and analysis to drive deep learning?	Frameworks to support systematic analysis will be helpful. This might involve training for staff. There will also need to be mechanisms to make learning explicit and shared to inform future enquiry.
6.	Does enquiry shape practice and practice shape enquiry such that it can be considered adaptive?	The link between practice and enquiry should be based on evidence collected. The questioning of this evidence by collaborators (or other audiences with whom findings are shared) should be at the heart of decision-making.
7.	Is enquiry informed by published research?	There is a place for teachers to be consumers of research and to access studies carried out in other contexts than their own, at different scales, to reveal insights. University partners or those studying at universities can access this body of work beyond that yet currently available open access.

The Ontario principles underpinning the questions above are explained in a monograph aimed at teaching professionals (Ontario Ministry of Education, 2010). It is available at: www.edu.gov.on.ca/eng/literacynumeracy/inspire/research/CBS_Collaborative_Teacher_Enquiry.pdf

They are also illustrated in action by the Brock University and Halton Region Collaborative Teacher Enquiry (2018) team in Ontario in relation to driving developments in technology-enhanced learning in primary schools. Further details of how each principle of collaborative teacher enquiry was led can be found at: www.knaer-recrae.ca/knowledge-hub/kmb-blog/9-tips-from-the-experts/383-a-collaborative-teacher-enquiry-into-makerspace-university-schools-learn-together

Useful websites

The Collaborative Action Research Network (CARN) is now an international network which covers collaborative action research not only in education, but also in health, social care, commercial and public services settings. It offers resources at: www.carn.org.uk/resources and supports the journal *Educational Action Research*.

The General Teaching Council of Scotland Practitioner Research webpage might also be of interest, especially the interactive 'What is practitioner enquiry?' wheel. It is available at: www.gtcs.org.uk/professional-update/research-practitioner-enquiry/practitioner-enquiry/what-is-practitioner-enquiry.aspx

The Teacher Education Advancement Network (TEAN) is a collaborative initiative, hosted and curated by the University of Cumbria for teacher education providers and associated organisations across the UK. It has a storehouse of resources and it is available at: www.cumbria.ac.uk/research/enterprise/tean/teachers-and-educators-storehouse

Chapter 5
Lesson Study as evidence-based teacher collaboration and enquiry

Haiyan Xu

5.1 Chapter overview

This chapter will outline:

5.2 the origins of interest in Lesson Study (LS) in the UK;

5.3 key variations in LS;

5.4 international evidence of the impact of LS on teacher and pupil learning;

5.5 practical illustrations of issues associated with LS;

5.6 challenges to consider when embedding LS in classrooms, schools and networks.

This chapter introduces Lesson Study (LS) and its international and local development in the UK since 2003. It draws on international evidence to illustrate the impact of LS on teacher and pupil learning outcomes. It discusses from a theoretical perspective what and how learning occurs in a LS context and exemplifies learning through illustrations drawn from Chinese and UK LS settings. The chapter ends with practical recommendations for practitioners, school leaders and network facilitators who intend to embed LS in their practice contexts.

5.2 The origins of interest of LS in the UK

LS first came to the attention of international educators and the classroom research community at the turn of the twenty-first century through Stigler and Hiebert's (1999) book *The Teaching Gap: Best Ideas From the World's Teachers for Improving Education in the Classroom*. In this book, the authors attribute the high performance of Japanese pupils in the Trends in International Mathematics and Science Study (TIMSS) to the fact that Japanese teachers engage in systemic LS practices. Since then LS has grown exponentially across the globe, with LS research and practice being developed in different cultural and educational contexts (Xu and Pedder, 2014). LS was introduced to

UK schools in 2003 by Pete Dudley in his capacity as the Director of National Strategies (Dudley, 2014). Since then, clusters of LS networks have grown in different parts of the country.

LS involves a group of teachers in iterative cycles of lesson planning, teaching/observation, evaluation and revision with the aim of enhancing the quality of classroom learning and the learning of pupils (Xu and Pedder, 2014). It brings together, within a shared and clear structure, opportunities for teachers not only to develop insights into their subject teaching and pupils' learning, but also to verify and embed those insights within the most germane unit of their everyday practice – the classroom lesson. Hence through engagement in LS, teachers can undertake a more continuous, collaborative and practice-based approach to teacher learning reported by many researchers as effective for enhancing teacher learning and classroom practice (Katsarou and Tsafos, 2008; Opfer and Pedder, 2011b; Schwille et al, 2007; Villegas-Reimers, 2003).

5.3 Key variations in LS

Procedure-wise, there is more than one way of undertaking LS. In countries like China and Japan, there is a national system and network in place to support LS activities at local, regional and national administrative levels of their school systems (Fernandez, 2002; Tsui and Wong, 2010). Rather than consistency, a wide range of LS variations have developed in both countries to meet different kinds and levels of professional learning and curriculum development need (Gu and Wang, 2003; Saito and Sato, 2012). Since the introduction of LS to the international community, other variations of LS have developed elsewhere to meet the specific needs of those country contexts. This chapter introduces the five variations most commonly discussed in published literature, so that the reader can decide which model or elements suit(s) their educational setting needs.

Chinese LS

In China teachers are usually organised by subject and year group into *Teaching Research Groups,* which are natural units of LS practice. Every week, half a day is set aside in school timetabling for these groups to engage in CPD activities, including LS. Additionally, it is typical for a school to include an LS month in every term plan. The key elements and steps of the Chinese model of LS are reflected in the diagram below (Figure 5a).

Typically, a full LS cycle includes three or more iterative cycles of research lesson development. It is usually the class teacher who teaches successive research lessons throughout the full cycle. The rationale for this is that the class teacher has more knowledge about their pupils and therefore can better realise the lesson plans.

Figure 5a Chinese model of LS

Identify an LS focus ⇩	This could be a specific area of curriculum, or a common pupil problem such as lack of motivation to learn.
Investigate the topic ⇩	This includes studying the curriculum, research literature or previous LS reports to know more about the topic.
Plan the lesson ⇩	This focuses on developing effective pedagogy for addressing the focal issue.
Teach and observe ⇩	The class teacher teaches the lesson and the others observe. The focus is on gathering evidence of pupil learning or not learning.
Review and revise ⇩	The group get together to evaluate what has or hasn't worked based on observation evidence. They refine the lesson plan.
Repeat the cycle ⇩	They teach and revise the lesson plan until they are satisfied that it effectively addresses the identified focus.
Write a report	The group reflect on the whole process and write a report on what they have developed and learned.

Other LS variations

The table below (Table 5a) introduces four other LS variations and summarises their key differences in procedures and rationale for use.

Table 5a A comparison of international LS variations

	Japanese LS	UK LS	Learning Study	Open House LS
Contexts for use	The most widely reported LS model in the literature.	The UK LS model (Dudley, 2011).	The Hong Kong LS model (Pang and Ling, 2011) but used in some European countries such as Sweden (Holmqvist, 2011).	An LS variation widely used in China and Japan (Saito, 2012; Huang et al, 2014). It includes two phases: lesson development and lesson dissemination.
Similarities	To Chinese LS in its rationale and procedures.	To the Japanese model in its procedures, but emphasises the importance of case pupils and pupil voice.	To the main procedures of Chinese LS but adopts the variation theory as a guiding pedagogical theory (see Pang and Marton, 2003).	The lesson development phase is similar to a cycle of LS.
Differences	Members of the LS group take turns to teach.	Plan, teach, observe and evaluate lessons around case pupils.	Use variation theory to inform lesson planning. Use pre- and post-tests to diagnose and evaluate learning.	Final lesson often taught live in front of a large audience to showcase new ideas or ways of realising the curriculum

	Japanese LS	UK LS	Learning Study	Open House LS
Key use	For those who are new to LS as it encourages shared ownership of the LS process.	For developing differentiated and personalised learning.	Pedagogical alternative. A more structured tool for action research.	For developing network learning.

5.4 International evidence of the impact of LS on teacher and pupil learning

LS is a tried and tested model of teacher collaboration and learning. An international review of 67 research studies on LS (2002–2013) revealed a wide evidence base of the impact of LS across a diverse range of cultural and educational contexts in Asia, Africa, the Middle East, Europe and America (Xu and Pedder, 2014). The institutional contexts reflected in these studies included the whole educational spectrum from pre-school to tertiary education and teacher education programmes, covering school subjects such as English, mathematics, science, languages, arts, geography and history.

These studies point consistently to four main areas of positive outcomes associated with teachers' engagement in LS, summarised in Table 5b (Xu and Pedder, 2014). These findings evidence its efficacy for enhancing the quality of teachers' learning, classroom teaching, and the learning of pupils in different cultural and educational contexts.

Table 5b Summary of the impact of LS

Reported impact	Weight of evidence	Evidence sources	Comments on the evidence	Examples of studies
1. Teacher collaboration and development of professional learning community	About a third of the studies	Teacher testimonials, researcher observation	Teachers develop collegiality, joint decision making, and joint ownership for teaching that leads to the cultivation of PLCs.	Lawrence and Chong, 2010 Sims and Walsh, 2009
2. Development of professional knowledge, practice and profession-alism	About a quarter of the studies	Teacher interviews, researcher observations, recordings of LS talk	Teachers develop a wide range of knowledge such as subject content knowledge, pedagogical knowledge, knowledge about pupils, knowledge about technology for teaching, and teachers' pedagogical content knowledge. This reinforces their identity as a teaching professional.	Dudley, 2013 Lee, 2008 Lewis, 2009 Ono et al, 2011

3. More explicit focus on pupil learning	About a third of the studies	Recordings of LS talk, researcher observation, teacher testimonials	Teachers shift their focus from teaching to learning and develop greater awareness and deeper insights about learners and their needs. They could better predict pupils' learning difficulties and formulate strategies to help them overcome barriers in learning.	Norwich and Ylonen, 2013 Perry and Lewis, 2009 Gao and Ko, 2009
4. Improved quality of classroom teaching and learning	About a third of the studies	Teacher testimonials, lesson recordings, pupil performance at high stake tests	Quality of classroom teaching improves in support of improvements in the quality of pupil learning. Schools that have practised LS for a few years have better pupil outcomes than other schools.	Ono and Ferreira, 2010 Robinson and Leikin, 2012

5.5 Practical illustrations of issues associated with LS

It is clear from the review of LS literature that its benefits affect different facets of personal and professional learning and development. This can be explained by different modes of social learning being at play when teachers collaborate in LS groups. Salomon and Perkins (1998, pp 4–6) provide a useful framework covering six modes of social learning in collaborative contexts and processes, which can be applied to LS. Consistent with the sociocultural tradition (Vygotsky, 1987), Salomon and Perkins (1998) hold that learning is first and foremost social. However, their theorisation of learning sustains an explicit balance between individual and collective facets of learning. Illustrations are offered from Chinese and UK schools to illuminate each of these pathways of learning.

Illustration 1: LS members helping another member to learn

Ying and her colleagues taught English as a foreign language in a Beijing primary school. They worked in an LS on the topic of eating in a restaurant. In the lesson planning, they came into disagreement about whether the sentence pattern for ordering food in a restaurant should be 'what would you like to eat?' or 'what do you like to eat?'. While Ying thought both could be used in this context, her colleague thought the former was more appropriate. She offered the reasoning that the former was to ask about choice at that particular moment, while the latter was about a general preference. This convinced Ying and they went on to plan the lesson using the former as the main language support. In this instance, Ying came to realise a subtle difference in language with the help of her colleague.

This illustration exemplifies Salomon and Perkins' (1998) first mode of social learning: *active social mediation of individual learning,* which takes place when a more experienced person or a team helps an individual to learn. In the LS context, this kind of learning is often facilitated by *'the knowledgeable other'* (Takahashi, 2014) such as a subject specialist who takes part in the LS as a critical friend or a more experienced teacher(s) supporting a less experienced or novice teacher to learn.

Illustration 2: members of the LS team learn together

Sue and two colleagues were primary school teachers in a London school. They did an LS to help their foundation level children to learn the concepts of 'half' and 'whole'. They first planned a paper-folding activity to help the pupils develop an experiential understanding of 'half' and 'whole'. They then moved on to reinforce their understanding by asking

them to identify halves from a range of images, starting with easy images such as a half-coloured circle to more complicated images such as a circle divided in six equal portions with every other portion coloured. The pupils could identify the easy ones but got stuck with the more difficult image. The teachers didn't initially predict that the pupils would get stuck here so didn't plan any further scaffolding activities except verbal explanation. After the lesson they felt that some pupils were still confused. So they came up with the idea of asking the pupils to cut the circle up into six portions and re-arrange them. They tried this in the next lesson and this time the pupils could clearly see that the image was indeed a half. In this LS, Sue and her colleagues learned about a difficult learning point for their pupils and developed a new idea to help them overcome the hurdle.

This illustration exemplifies Salomon and Perkins' (1998) second mode of social learning: *social mediation as participatory knowledge co-construction,* which takes place when a group of people work in collaboration to learn something new. In this illustration, the group forms a collective learning system where learning is co-constructed and shared. (Also see Butler et al, 2008).

Illustration 3: learning from external resources such as research

Catherine and her two colleagues were primary teachers in a London school with a high proportion of pupils from disadvantaged backgrounds. A common problem that they faced was their pupils' lack of language skills to explain reasoning and develop thinking and group learning. They decided to do an LS to address this problem. As part of their investigation of the LS focus, they came across Mercer's (1995) theory of exploratory talk and a set of group-talk protocols which they decided to try in their LS.

In Lesson 1, they found that pupils were good at taking turns and being respectful, but not so good at listening and responding to what other children said.

In Lesson 2, they specifically modelled *building on* someone's idea and *challenging* someone's idea respectfully and provided the pupils with sentence prompts. The children found the modelling very helpful and were able to contribute and engage more in the group discussion.

In Lesson 3, they focused on developing the skills to identify *which* skill to use and *when* by giving each child a particular skill to listen out for and modelling this skill when necessary. The pupils engaged even more actively this time and could talk about the skills in a reflective manner.

This illustration typifies Salomon and Perkins' (1998) third mode of social learning: *social mediation by cultural scaffolding,* with learning mediated by cultural tools. In the LS context, this is often reflected in the kind of learning when teachers study curriculum guidance, materials or the research literature as part of their investigation of an LS focus.

Illustration 4: learning as a team

Alex worked in a London secondary school where he headed the maths department. The six members of the department generally got along with each other. But Alex felt that there was little discourse about teaching and learning outside the formal departmental meetings. He wanted to try LS and managed to persuade two other colleagues to join him. They then extended the LS to the whole department and invited others to take part in the lesson observation and evaluation. This generated enthusiastic and stimulating discussions about the lesson and the kind of typical difficulties and misconceptions that they observed. After that all the other teachers agreed to take part in LS. They developed some interesting findings through each LS and decided that the findings should inform the school scheme of learning. In the meantime, there were also more informal exchanges of thoughts and ideas among the department on a daily basis. It seems that, as a group, they not only found a structured way to work together, but had also changed their culture.

This illustration depicts Salomon and Perkins' (1998) fourth mode of social learning: *the social entity as a learning system.* In an LS context this might be where a team such as a group of subject teachers learn collectively as a social entity through critically evaluating and reflecting on current practices and procedures, developing new understandings, skills and practices, and hence learning how to function better as a team.

Illustration 5: learning social skills to deal with conflicts and maximise learning

In the same LS cycle as discussed in Illustration 1, Ying and her colleagues had opposing views on what a review lesson on the topic of eating in a restaurant would look like. Ying proposed a focus on content while her colleague Lan proposed a focus on context. Because they each held firmly to their own ideas, they used their speech turns to assert and build upon their own ideas, rather than engaging substantially with what the other had to say. The tension built up to the point when everybody stopped talking and there was a sustained period of silence. Perhaps having reflected on this episode, Ying broke the silence and asked Lan to further clarify her ideas. They all listened to each other this time. As a team they were able to develop a plan that incorporated both content and context, for example asking pupils to create menus as a way to review vocabulary, to listen to food-ordering conversations and select customer choices on the menu like a waiter, and to act out the food-ordering scenario in groups. In this LS, it seemed that the teachers of this group were able to reflect in situ and develop better ways of talking to each other to save the LS from the brink of failure to a success.

This illustration illuminates Salomon and Perkins' (1998) fifth form of social learning: *learning to be a social learner,* which refers to the development of practical capacities that enable an individual to identify and draw on social resources skilfully to take full advantage of a particular learning opportunity.

Illustration 6: learning what helps a team to learn

David and two colleagues worked in LS cycles as part of a research project based in Camden Borough to look at the impact of LS on developing higher order mathematical thinking among pupils. In this project they were asked to video-record their LS meetings. After they completed the first LS cycle, they attended a workshop covering the key ground rules for talk in LS, such as 'everyone is encouraged to contribute', 'everyone is prepared to accept challenge', 'alternatives are discussed before reaching a decision'. The group then reviewed their own LS videos with the set of ground rules in mind and realised that participation was not necessarily equally distributed and that sometimes an idea was accepted without exploring alternatives. Having developed such awareness about the way they talked in the first LS cycle, they decided that they would pay particular attention to encouraging everyone to contribute and exploring alternatives more in their next LS cycle.

This illustration demonstrates Salomon and Perkins' (1998) sixth mode of social learning: *learning social content,* which emphasises the importance of developing awareness of the social processes which support learning, learning such skills as developing interpersonal relationships and establishing solidarity and trust in groups. This is essential for making members of an LS group feel safe to share their personal views and sometimes ignorance as opportunities for learning.

Given the many facets of individual and collective learning that can take place through LS, it is no wonder that it has been sustained in countries like China and Japan for many decades and that, since its introduction in the English medium two decades ago, is being taken up worldwide.

5.6 Challenges of LS

Despite the benefits and opportunities for learning offered by LS, there have been reports of challenges and constraints with this practice. The most frequently mentioned challenges, unsurprisingly, are time and extra workload (Lee, 2008). A second challenge, however, is the lack of strong leadership support to create favourable conditions for teachers to adopt and sustain LS practice (Meng and Sam, 2011). Furthermore, tension or conflict can arise during the challenging process of changing from a private, individualistic and sometimes competitive culture towards a collaborative culture and can deem collaboration fruitless (Puchner and Taylor, 2006). On the other hand, cultural tendencies to avoid conflict in some contexts can be similarly obstructive for genuine productive collaboration to take place (Perry and Lewis, 2009). In some cases, a culture of prioritising accountability and exams can prevent teachers from shifting their mindset from teaching to learning (Saito et al, 2008, 2012). It is therefore important that school leaders and policymakers who are keen to embed LS be aware of the potential challenges and come up with counter strategies in order to maximise the benefits of LS.

5.7 Summary

LS as a particular form of JPD has travelled internationally. Different variants have developed with some of these covered as they developed in key national contexts to offer a richer appreciation of how it has been operationalised. LS is a complex tool to lead but can be powerful for individual teachers as well as for their schools, as exemplified through concrete illustrations in this chapter. Chapter 6 illustrates how LS was used by school leaders to try to develop professional learning communities in two UK settings.

Table 5c

Key actions as an LS team	Why is this important? What is important?
Ground rules for LS talk (based on Mercer (1995), Dudley (2013) and Xu (2016)) • All members of the LS group are equal as learners • Everyone in the group is encouraged to contribute • All contributions are treated with respect • All members will share what they know, what they think and why • All members will listen to each other and build on the discussion • All members will be prepared to accept challenges • All members will discuss alternatives but will seek to reach an agreement as a group • All members will share what they learn and with colleagues and pupils appropriately	This is to make sure that the LS process is shared and owned by each member of the group.
Key actions as a school to embed LS	**Why is this important? What is important?**
Success factors (based on LSEF Camden Higher Order Mathematics LS project) • Strong leadership support and involvement in LS • LS leads who are knowledgeable about LS process and passionate about developing this practice	When these conditions are met, it is more likely that LS will embed and sustain at the school level.

• Prioritising LS to other CPD obligations for teachers • Using LS to replace traditional performance management • Linking LS with school development priorities	
Key actions for developing LS networks	**Why is this important?** **What is important?**
Success factors (based on LSEF Camden Higher Order Mathematics LS project) • Local LS leads who have experience in LS can become lead professional in a subject • Develop a curriculum focus as shared LS focus in order to coordinate the LS efforts and develop deeper learning • Make sure that expertise among the network is identified and shared • Make sure that leadership support and commitment is sought and guaranteed from each school • Use a variety of ways to share learning, such as presentations, case studies, video documentation of key learning points, and Open House LS	These factors help LS networks to become self-sufficient and self-sustaining communities of practice.

Exploring further

Dudley, P (ed) (2014) *Lesson Study: Professional Learning For Our Time.* London: Routledge. This book introduces LS and draws on an international review of LS research studies. It covers successful examples of LS from the UK and Japan, including examples of using LS to address learners with special educational needs.

International Journal of Learning and Lesson Studies. This online journal is the official journal of the World Association of Lesson Study (WALS) (www. emeraldgrouppublishing.com/products/journals/journals.htm?id=ijlls). It publishes the latest developments in LS research and case studies from all over the world, with an ongoing call for studies in the form of action research, design experiments, formative evaluations or pedagogical research.

Useful Websites

LSUK: www.lessonstudy.co.uk. This website offers free resources for download such as an LS handbook and workbook that include a step-by-step guide on how to undertake LS. It also provides links to LS networks and projects in the UK, including the LSEF-funded Camden Higher Order Mathematics projects.

WALS: www.walsnet.org. The World Association of Lesson Study holds an annual conference each year, which has been held in countries such as Singapore, Hong Kong, Sweden, China, the UK and Indonesia attracting 800–1000 international teaching professionals and university researchers. The website also holds webinars by international LS experts on a regular basis.

Chapter 6
Leading professional learning communities: opportunities and challenges

Geoff Baker

6.1 Chapter overview

This chapter will outline:

6.2   the challenges inherent in balancing visions against the realities of developing PLCs;

6.3   reflections on a voluntary approach to developing a PLC (case study 1);

6.4   reflections on a whole-school approach to developing a PLC (case study 2);

6.5   the case for school leaders to utilise PLCs as a model for teacher development.

This chapter examines *professional learning communities (PLCs)*, from the perspective of a school leader. It offers an exploration of the challenges inherent in utilising PLCs as a model for teacher development. While being grounded in recent literature, this chapter illustrates the experiences of implementing two alternative PLC approaches to teacher development, as experienced by the author. These two case studies highlight the strength of PLC in promoting teacher collaboration and encouraging teachers to adopt evidence-based practices, at the same time as noting alternatives and practical issues for school leaders. So prevalent has work on PLCs become, that critics have complained that a 'new orthodoxy' has arisen such that, while PLCs are accepted as having the power to transform professions, they are rarely talked about with precision (Amin and Roberts, 2008). PLCs are complex phenomena (Levine, 2010). In practice they can develop organically, occurring naturally when colleagues work closely together, as well as being associated with activities and structures contrived by an organisation's leadership. Even when contrived, they are likely to be articulated in different ways. It is also possible for individual practitioners to be part of multiple communities, some that may be officially and artificially constructed within the work environment and others that may be the result of informal connections. As a consequence of the growth of interest in PLCs as presented in Chapter 2 (Little, 2002; Palincsar, 1999; Stoll and Louis, 2007), literature has emerged that provides practical guidance on how to support and grow effective communities. This includes advice about how to structure professional communities, what kinds of things they should discuss and how they should share their findings (DuFour and DuFour, 2012; Graham and Ferriter, 2010; Hord and Sommers, 2008).

6.2 The challenges inherent in balancing visions against the realities of developing PLCs

Grossman et al (2000, p 942) have critiqued PLCs as a meaningless buzzword and an *'obligatory appendage to every educational innovation'*. PLCs rely on sound relationship building, a vision and leadership practice which establishes supportive culture of trust. Despite the advice on how to structure PLCs, they are not straightforward to establish. While PLCs can foster creativity and celebrate good practice, it is equally possible that, for a variety of reasons, they can also stifle innovation and affirm practice that falls below a standard those outside the community might deem acceptable, leading to inertia (McLaughlin and Talbert, 2001; Wenger and Synder, 2000; Talbert, 2010). For this reason, any initiative grounded in the notion of a PLC must ensure that the community is outward looking to ensure that existing ideas about practice are challenged (McLaughlin and Talbert, 2001).

The following two case studies draw on teachers using LS, as covered in Chapter 5, with the aim of developing PLCs within a school. The two schools illustrate different approaches to community-building: the first based on invitation and voluntary participation, the second a school-wide initiative involving all teachers. The two approaches taken were studied in parallel to address three key questions.

1. What values does a PLC model of teacher development have for participants and other stakeholders?

2. To what extent are individual learning processes enhanced through participation in PLCs?

3. How far do different approaches towards PLC models of teacher development impact on the outcomes of involvement?

6.3 PLCs for teacher development through voluntary participation

One possible practical approach to PLC-building for teacher development, and hence school improvement, is illustrated by a project undertaken at a small comprehensive secondary school in England. This involved three triads completing an LS project following a UK interpretation of LS (Lewis and Hurd, 2011; Dudley, 2011, 2013) – see Chapter 5.

The project's design

As school leader of this secondary school I led the project as a piece of practitioner research. This involved a research design in which all participants, along with school leaders involved in the process, engaged in a semi-structured interview before and after the experience, designed to evaluate the project's success.

In this project LS involved triads of three colleagues from different subject areas volunteering to collaborate on developing a single lesson for students (aged 11–12) – the subject area chosen was one that all members of the triad thought they could access. A member of the triad then delivered the lesson, while being observed by the other two members of the triad, and the lesson then developed in light of the observation and the feedback from students and teachers. This process was repeated three times such that each member of the triad had taught a version of the lesson. A key aspect of the approach was that at the start of the project all involved chose and engaged with a piece of research from a peer-reviewed source to contextualise the intervention in pedagogical research.

The above process was presented to all teachers at the school to ask for voluntary participation, with an awareness that to make this mandatory might have led to feelings of distrust, lack of engagement and lack of authenticity and that only superficial change which would be hard to sustain might result (Opfer and Pedder, 2011a; Goodnough, 2011). From a staff of 34 teachers, nine teachers volunteered.

The findings

Despite explaining the intention that those colleagues who took part would genuinely own the process, all who became involved noted feelings of anxiety about participation. Within the school there were generally good relationships between teachers and leaders, so the one issue that emerged around trust, 'I am a little bit worried that the headteacher will find out if I teach a bad lesson'

(Maya), was easy to dispel by making it clear that participants in the triads were responsible for deciding what, if anything, was shared with school leaders. Far harder to dispel were the initial concerns that participants had about opening up their classroom to external scrutiny from their peers, a fear that appeared more acute the longer the participant had been teaching. 'I have been teaching for many years now and only ever have other teachers in my room when it is one of my yearly observations – I think I am a good teacher, but it is hard letting your friends and work colleagues into your classroom' (Tabitha). Freda referred to the classroom as typically a 'secret space'. Underlying the notion of PLCs and the LS approach adopted was a clear aim to open up classrooms and get colleagues to collaborate. Although the teachers were excited about being involved in the project, this philosophy challenged the status quo. Significantly however, despite these initial concerns, feedback at the end of the project highlighted collaboration as the most beneficial aspect of being involved in the project.

One of the clearest impacts of participation in the project was the contribution it made to a change of ethos in the school. All participants quickly adapted to having colleagues in the room with them, watching them teach and providing feedback. Ahmed noted it as 'liberating'. Greta reflected that 'It was strange... Before doing this we all agreed a scheme of work, we all taught the skills and knowledge for the same exam and we all marked each other's papers, so how strange to then close ourselves off ... not letting each other into our rooms'. A philosophical rethinking about collaborative approaches to teaching was underpinned by a recognition of the usefulness of having collegial collaboration. All participants reported how this enhanced their own practice. Freda stated that 'the comments [of a colleague] were so useful – they told me how they would use different strategies to question students, really basic stuff like asking for hands up, choosing volunteers and making a game of it by using a name generator on the computer ... that way they got all students involved all of the time'. Tomas noted that 'I didn't realise it but I often turn my back to the class when giving feedback, which meant that I was shutting myself off from the rest of the group'.

The recognition of the value of this kind of collaboration had a physical impact on the school. While hard to measure, it was noted that windows onto corridors which had once been covered with posters were cleared and doors that were once shut became left open and welcoming. This in turn had a broader impact on the whole school. This change was perhaps most evident when, following completion of this project, colleagues were all invited to take part and encouraged to form triads, using directed time for the process or to complete other teacher-led enquiry. No doubt, largely as a result of how positively participants in the project felt, every member of staff opted to participate.

Not only did colleagues become enthusiastic about collaborating to improve their practice, but it also created a clear research culture within the school.

A key element of the project was that participants engaged with pedagogical literature that focused on some aspect relating to the lesson that they would be teaching. Participants were unanimously concerned about this aspect of the project: 'I have not read any research about teaching and learning since I left university 12 years ago. Not sure I will understand it' (Freda); 'I get watching staff, but I am not sure that a journal article is really going to be helpful. Is this just box ticking?' (Greta). However, from feedback interviews, engaging with the literature was perceived as one of the most useful parts of the project: 'Really enjoyed the readings. They were relevant and made me think about things in a very different way' (Maya); 'While challenging, it is good to think about the latest ideas in the field' (Ahmed). Perhaps the most interesting piece of feedback was from Greta, who had initially been sceptical: 'Actually found the article very helpful and spent a few hours looking up other relevant stuff ... thinking about it, if we hadn't done this, we wouldn't have had anything new to discuss' (Greta). This view accords with published evidence about PLCs, which reports that new ideas help stimulate discussions and challenge existing assumptions and practice (McLaughlin and Talbert, 2001). The impact of this was seen in the multiple requests from participants who completed the project to purchase books about teaching and learning or who then joined subject associations.

An even more surprising outcome of the project was that it stimulated a research culture not only among the staff participating, but also – participants believed – among the students. While the project interviews had initially focused on the attitudes and understanding of colleagues taking part, in the second interviews, a number specifically alluded to the impact of the relationship between teachers and students and how they perceived the classroom environment differently as a result. In accordance with ethically sound practice, students in the classes that were taught as part of the triads were told that staff were engaged in a project to develop their teaching and that three teachers would be teaching the same lesson to three different groups. This caused teachers some initial trepidation: 'I was worried that the kids would see this as an opportunity to muck around, particularly as they knew that I was not teaching my own subject' (Frank). Far from it. All participants who mentioned the attitude of the students reported that they found it 'exciting' (Ahmed), 'fun' (Tabitha) and 'it felt like we were on the same team as we were all thinking about what could make the lesson better' (Frank). Maria noted, 'the children seemed, to me at least, so interested as they had a voice in what was happening to them ... they had been empowered'.

6.4 PLCs for teacher development as a whole-school strategy

The second case study was based in a high performing sixth-form college. The project followed a similar pattern to the first case study in that three colleagues worked together to plan a lesson, which was observed by the remaining members of the triad. The lesson was developed in light of feedback and the process was repeated until all three members had delivered the lesson. There was also the requirement that, during the course of planning a particular lesson, participants engaged with a piece of relevant pedagogical research, in a bid to bring new ideas and fresh perspectives. There were, however, two key differences between the case studies based on the strategic approach taken by the college's leadership.

The project's design

Firstly, in case study 2 all three members of each triad were purposely taken from the *same* subject area. Secondly, *every* teacher in the college was instructed to take part in the LS programme as part of their directed time. There was no option for colleagues not to take part and complete a different activity. It was designed in this way to allow equity of access to the outcomes of the project across the college and to offer a form of CPD for all staff. Semi-structured interviews were completed with all participants from three randomly-chosen triads, along with the principal of the college.

The findings

A key feature of the first interviews was a level of anxiety about taking part in LS. Steve stated that the approach was 'unusual – I am not sure how helpful it is going to be for me to have my friends watch me teach … if anything it is going to cause me anxiety I don't need'. Shania felt that the approach 'might be good as I have more experienced people in my team, but I am not sure how an NQT could have the authority needed to offer useful comments'. David was particularly negative, feeling that 'this is the latest fad and I would be much better using the time to mark and plan'. Others were more enthusiastic, believing it might be a 'good way to get new ideas' (Graeme) or that it 'will make me think more about my own teaching' (Lydia). Even the principal, who was leading the LS programme, noted some concerns – 'from my research I know this is a great way to get teachers to improve, but they need to go into it with the right mindset and be positive about it, which I am not sure everyone is' (Andrea). Certainly, there was a much larger spectrum of responses in case study two, which was no doubt a reflection of the fact that participants were not volunteers.

Despite the initial trepidation towards the project, on completion the majority of participants identified ways in which the project had positively impacted on their teaching. Toby noted that students had observed a colleague who 'had very high expectations of every student and they seemed to step up ... since seeing this I have demanded more from my classes and they have not let me down yet'. Shania, initially sceptical, reflected: 'I have seen a lot of ideas that I am going to ruthlessly steal and bring into my own lessons'. The notion of taking ideas from colleagues was the most frequently positive reflection: 'Getting ideas from another member of staff teaching is similar to reading a book about different ways of teaching a lesson' (Anha). The other aspect of the project that participants appeared to value was discussing conclusions from pedagogical research. As with case study 1, it led one participant to request funds to create a departmental library that focused on teaching methods. While there was a lot of positivity about LS after the project was completed, there were still concerns about its design.

A key difference between this case study and the first is that the triads consisted of participants from the same subject area. Indeed, participants questioned whether it would be meaningful at all to work with someone from a different subject area. David questioned, 'how can a PE teacher offer meaningful comments about teaching in my subject?' Having completed the LS, Shania felt that working with experienced subject specialists had been useful – 'they had both been teaching for much longer, so it was interesting to see what they thought about how to teach the actual topic ... they had real depth of subject knowledge that I don't currently have'. While this was seen as a positive, limitations were also noted: 'In my field we are all similar types of people and all seem to teach in a similar way' (Lydia); 'It would have been nice to see something a bit more different, to take me out of my comfort zone ... it was a great experience, but I wasn't really challenged' (Graeme).

A striking aspect of the feedback from case study 2 was that the participants seemed to largely view it as another, limited type of CPD, as opposed to leading to any change in culture or ethos within the school. For instance, the majority of participants indicated that, despite having enjoyed aspects of the programme, they would not voluntarily complete another cycle of LS. One participant summed up their view of this by stating 'it was interesting, but there is better CPD that doesn't require as much effort' (Sean). When pressed on what such CPD might be, Sean concluded that 'traditional lectures about how to teach' were preferable. Anya, who again had a lot of positives to share about the approach, felt that the experience of LS could be 'invasive' as it meant that others had the opportunity to critique your views and practice and this could lead to 'resentment'. In all cases participants were unable to articulate any specific reason for feeling like this, but the general theme seemed to be how the LS was introduced and conceptualised at that school. While all took positives from the experience, LS had not led to a change in school culture in ways more clearly evidenced in case study 1.

6.5 The case for school leaders to utilise PLCs as a model for teacher development

While impossible to isolate the discrete impact of the project, after completion both schools reported improved student outcomes and Ofsted judgements. Leaders in both settings felt that participants left the project with enhanced professional knowledge about how to teach and an enhanced knowledge of their students. On a more practical level Toby, a senior teacher, noted this as 'the cheapest teacher development but... the most meaningful CPD' they had ever utilised.

There was divergence in the significance of the outcomes between the different case-study projects. In case study 1, the project led to a ground swell of interest in teaching and learning with one leader noting that, for the first time, they felt the school had begun to move towards a self-sustaining model of improvement. The importance of the students feeling part of a real research project was felt to be critical to the movement of the school towards one 'where everyone learns and where everyone has a respected voice in improving that experience ... as bizarre as it may seem I think participation in the project brought staff and students to life' (Toby). They also noted an improvement in student behaviour which felt attributable to this shift.

In case study 2, while still having had a largely positive impact on participants, the more radical nature of the model appeared to have been missed, with the majority of participants expressing reluctance to become involved again. Implications for leaders are in both the manner of recruitment and the structuring of the JPD groupings. Case study 2 reflected the 'contrived collegiality' identified by many commentators as being a potentially limiting factor in professional community development (Datnow, 2011). Likewise, while the approach utilised in case study 2 in which all participants were from the same discipline meant that there was more opportunity for subject-specific discourse, this was reported to have limited creativity within the triads.

6.6 Summary

This enquiry-based chapter has compared two different approaches towards PLC-building and illustrated the concerns and benefits. Both approaches showed the potential for Lesson Study as a form of JPD to be beneficial to teachers' development. While the project on which the chapter was based was initially focused on participating teachers' perceptions and reported experiences, the feedback from teachers and anecdotal evidence in case study 1 revealed the potential to gain broader benefits to students and school ethos. This offered more tangible PLC building and indeed moved towards a sense of whole-school learning community. The two case studies contrast alternative leadership approaches, which shed light on the greater challenges to introducing collaborative enquiry approaches when made mandatory across an educational setting. Both case studies show how initial concerns from participants can be dramatically overturned and how teachers can fundamentally change mindset and practice to being more open to learning from others, not only from within their context, but also from wider published literature. Challenges and opportunities for teachers in accessing and using such published evidence are explored in Chapter 7.

Questions for enquiry in your own school

The following questions might guide leaders in thinking about a strategic approach to instigating and supporting PLCs particularly linked to the two alternatives offered in this chapter.

- Will a volunteer or 'conscripted' approach to teacher development work best in your school, and why?

- Can you identify potential teaching and learning champions would could pilot an LS (or other JPD) approach and then share their experiences with the rest of the school?

- Do you want to deepen subject knowledge by having LS triads made up of participants from the same subject, or foster creativity by having multi-disciplinary triads?

Exploring further

For a fuller discussion of conceptualisations of professional communities, the following synthesis is recommended.

Levine, T H (2010) Tools for the Study and Design of Collaborative Teacher Learning: The Affordances of Different Conceptions of Teacher Community and Activity Theory. *Teacher Education Quarterly*, 37(1): 109–30.

For a view of collaboration and contrived collegiality an excellent starting point is: Hargreaves, A (1994) *Changing Teachers, Changing Times: Teachers' Work and Culture in the Postmodern Age*. London: Cassell.

This has been more recently critiqued:

Datnow, A (2011) Collaboration and Contrived Collegiality: Revisiting Hargreaves in the Age of Accountability. *Journal of Educational Change*, 12(2): 147–58.

Chapter 7
Teachers' access to and use of evidence

Eric Addae-Kyeremeh

7.1 Chapter overview

This chapter will outline:

7.2   an introduction to the issues associated with teachers' access to evidence;

7.3   key challenges and benefits of teachers accessing published evidence;

7.4   the range and forms of evidence to which teachers have access;

7.5   how teachers can be critical in the selection and use of evidence;

7.6   the role of social media and social networking for teachers' professional learning;

7.7   case studies illustrating teachers as consumers of evidence.

7.2 Introduction and key issues associated with teachers' access to evidence

The call since the 1990s, especially in the UK, for educational practice to become more *'evidence-based'* – or more recently *'evidence-informed'* (Coldwell et al, 2017) – is arguably not a new phenomenon. After all, has education practice not always been informed by evidence? In the school setting evidence is often generated by teachers as part of an investigation into some aspect of work – looking at, for example, the impact of changes of teaching on the learning of the pupils as measured through their achievements, attitudes etc. It may be looking at the impact of new approaches to presenting lessons, to changing classroom groupings or layout, to styles of questioning or modes of assessment. Alternatively, it might be enquiring into a part of everyday practice which has been carried out rather implicitly and onto which a 'spotlight' is to be shone. For example, if a teacher wishes to observe more systematically the behaviours or interactions of certain groups of pupils, or the way particular resources are used.

As argued in Chapter 4, instead of looking to their own evidence, teachers and more broadly educational practitioners, are increasingly referred to externally generated sources (Goldacre, 2013a, 2013b). This has come without the offer of support for evaluating and interrogating the evidence available to them, which would allow practitioners to critically evaluate how to apply such evidence to their practice contexts. This is accompanied by the danger of restricting teachers' access to the broader research evidence available, particularly that in the form of academic publications.

This chapter focuses on teachers as consumers of evidence and covers the range and forms of evidence to which teachers have access. It reflects on how drawing on sources of evidence external to their context requires teachers and educators to be critical in their choice and judgement of what might be applicable to their contexts. Thoughts are offered as to how to evaluate and appraise different forms of evidence available and reflections included about new ways to engage with academic research across professional and academic boundaries using social networking for teachers' professional learning. Case studies of teachers engaging with evidence to inform practice are included.

7.3 Key challenges and benefits of teachers accessing published evidence

The following quotes illustrate evidence-based arguments about the challenges (to the right) and the benefits (to the left) of teachers acting as consumers of published research.

How do teachers know which practices are effective, which to change and which are worth trying? Teachers need an evidence base to draw upon. Should such evidence be developed themselves from local enquiry or adopted and adapted from published research? Both are powerful sources towards evidence-informed practice but require time to engage with.

(Stenhouse, 1981; Elliott, 2004; Cain et al, 2016; Philpott and Poultney, 2018)

The whole profession needs to develop the mindset of continual renewal and critique of its knowledge-base, to be in constant enquiry, which is closer to the vision and practice found in the medical profession. Arguably, if enquiry is not the vision for teaching, should teaching be called a profession?

(Hargreaves, D, 1994; Day and Sachs, 2004)

> There is no time to read academic papers or to engage in enquiry in the current busy school. There is no capacity for leaders to find time to create space in a weekly timetable for teachers to meet together.

(See et al, 2016; Bloom, 2016)

> A vision is needed which requires a shared understanding by the school community of the importance of collaboratively developed knowledge. This should involve looking both inward and outward, including to partners and published sources of evidence.

(McLaughlin and Black-Hawkins, 2004; McLaughlin and Talbert, 2007; Stoll et al, 2006; 2018)

7.4 The range and forms of evidence to which teachers have access

The Oxford dictionary definition of evidence refers to *'The available body of facts or information indicating whether a belief or proposition is true or valid'* (Lexico.com, 2019). What you consider as *'true'* or *'valid,'* however, depends on your world view of the social world, such as of education. It is helpful to think about evidence as the wealth of information and data types used to support or contradict claims made about what counts as knowledge or to test a hypothesis about how something works or might work. In these ways, evidence can inform what teachers know, believe and do (Saunders, 2015). To engage with evidence and to apply it to practice therefore requires teachers to reflect on what constitutes reliable and/or valuable evidence and who makes that judgement.

So, what evidence counts as valuable?

When we talk about 'valuable evidence' in an educational setting, the debate revolves around new ideas, information and knowledge that can help shape and/or transform practice. In the practice of teachers, this will involve pedagogy, subject knowledge, subject-specific pedagogy, as well as procedural and practical knowledge about teaching in a specific school setting and/or even age range. Judgements about what can be considered valuable is therefore contextual, which also raises questions about scalability and replicability. For example, to what extent can evidence generated in a small-scale study be reliable enough to allow its adoption and implementation at a systems level? Or to what extent could evidence generated in highly resourced education systems be replicable in lower-resourced situations? The importance of these questions has led to policymakers favouring some forms of evidence-gathering over others, as discussed in Chapters 2 and 4, prioritising funding to quantitative and systematic studies such as RCTs.

While such approaches are welcomed by the education community, research evidence is only one piece of the evidence-informed jigsaw. Other forms of evidence include classroom data, teachers' own professional judgement and school-level data, which can all be valuable and mobilised to inform practice (Nelson and Campbell, 2017). Some academics (eg Biesta, 2015; Brown et al, 2017; Hammersley, 2005) advocate that evidence generated by practitioners for practitioners (usually small-scale and weighted to qualitative approaches) should be considered of equal value to that generated by the larger, quantitative approaches.

So, to what evidence do teachers have access?

Using the teachers' practice setting and level of interaction with evidence as a unit of analysis, Figure 7a represents three levels of access to evidence: micro, meso and macro.

Figure 7a Evidence pyramid

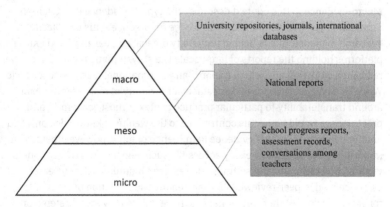

University repositories, journals, international databases

National reports

School progress reports, assessment records, conversations among teachers

macro

meso

micro

Micro-evidence in this context describes forms of evidence that are easily and readily available to the teacher and educator. These range from what teachers generate through everyday practice to that arising through formal and informal conversations with peers. These forms of contextual evidence concern *'knowledge in practice'*, held by teachers and their peers about what they have come to *'know' 'works'* (Lytle and Cochran-Smith, 1992). The search for micro-evidence is often triggered by teacher curiosity, for example wanting to know whether or how a new approach to teaching a topic has affected the achievement of pupils. The nature of this type of school-based study is that practice can be problematised and looked at critically. The starting point could be a challenge or problem but could also be a wish to shed light on the experiences of pupils as they study a particular topic. Professional conversations and discussions that take place among peers are also known to provide a wealth of micro-evidence valued by practitioners (Cooper et al, 2017).

Meso-evidence in this context goes beyond the classroom and includes evidence available at school and regional level, to which teachers often only have indirect or filtered access compared with the types of micro-evidence described earlier. This type of evidence is often predicated on the practice of others within similar educational contexts. Schools provide a range of reports to form the basis of regional and national data sets that makes comparative analysis possible, eg evidence about progression through Key Stages (in England) for 'disadvantaged' groups and aimed at informing future planning for improving the inclusivity of teaching and learning opportunities. In England, as elsewhere, the generation of evidence about 'good practice' (Fielding et al, 2005) has become a feature of the professional development landscape and, as outlined in previous chapters, school networks are sharing various forms of evidence (Stoll et al, 2012).

Macro-evidence in this context describes the type of evidence that Cochran-Smith and Lytle (1999) refer to as *'knowledge for practice'*. This is typically 'research evidence' that is held in university databases, peer-reviewed journals, platforms holding the reports of large-scale trials, systematic reviews and other published work that are held in national and international research repositories. While this type of evidence is contestable for a variety of reasons, principally around transferability to particular practice contexts, most academics and practitioners would agree this contributes to the wealth of knowledge on, about and for education. For this evidence to influence practice however, there is an important issue about how easily accessible such evidence is to practitioners working outside university settings and research institutes. Most research evidence held in peer-reviewed journals requires subscription or payments for access which teachers are unlikely to have unless they are registered on courses as a university student or their Alliance/Trust of schools has invested in subscriptions.

The move towards opening access to academic evidence will be an important one to resolve this barrier, but one which some call for being further researched itself (Knox, 2013). Abstracts are usually made available via a university's research repository (eg ORO: from the Open University). Open-access journals are gaining some momentum, which makes more research evidence available at no cost. There is also some movement around virtual communal sharing, where researchers are independently making their work freely available through social media spaces and independent web portals for practitioners and academics, eg Research Gate, BERA blogs, CollectivED, TEAN, Academia.edu. There is still a long way to go to make more research evidence open and freely available to schools, their staff and partners.

Evidence-informed practice is not simply about access to evidence or top-down advocation of particular forms of evidence and this book so far has presented the case for teachers to be active producers of evidence, systematically engaging with evidence through active experimentation and reflection with the aim of transforming practice. This chapter argues that part of this enquiry will be through consuming evidence as long as this involves enactment as well as evidence seeking. It is therefore imperative that teachers are critical in their appraisal of any evidence particularly research evidence to ascertain its applicability to their practice and their professional context.

7.5 Being critical in the appraisal and use of evidence

Most published 'empirical' research follows a structure which breaks the report into parts aligned to the conventions of academic research. A journal paper reporting an empirical study typically starts with an abstract, then locates the study in the wider literature, outlines the research design followed by a presentation and discussion of the evidence collected, ending with a conclusion, references and acknowledgements. This can be abbreviated as an IMRAD structure, which refers to *Introduction, Methods, Results, Analysis and Discussion* sections.

The abstracts for papers can serve as a useful summary of a paper and, as noted earlier, are more readily accessible than the full papers. They should provide a concise summary of the study's aims, methods, results and conclusions. However, to critically appraise a research study, it is necessary to read about the study in more detail to gain a good understanding of what it entailed. Just because a study has been published does not necessarily mean that it is unbiased or cannot be critiqued.

The following five-step process is offered as a useful guide for critical appraisal of research evidence as part of practitioner enquiry.

A five-step process for filtering/appraising research evidence

Step 1: Identify and evaluate the underpinning 'world view'

Readers of studies should first consider the underlying assumptions of the evidence being evaluated. One facet of this is described as the authors' 'world view' which underpins the focus, nature and reporting of any study. Sometimes these assumptions are implicit rather than explicit but it is useful to look for indications as to why a study has been carried out in a particular way. For some there will be an absolute truth that research is attempting to reveal which dictates a research design; eg a scientific method. Such a world view is described in research as 'positivist' and is often associated with gathering numeric data on large-scale samples and deploying statistical methods in the analysis. This is also a state of mind. Through an experimental design researchers try to find out what is happening with the aim of arriving at an answer or solution they believe is repeatable and reproducible. With this, there comes a danger that research might attempt to find 'the answer'.

On the other hand, researchers may adopt a completely different approach with a recognition that whatever they have set out to investigate is subject to interpretation. Such an 'interpretivist' approach would not seek to reveal an absolute truth and would not claim to do so, but instead presents interpretations from a set of data, as appears to be justifiable by the researcher. This type of research is often associated with data that represents people's attitudes and perceptions, often included in studies interrogating the complex practices associated with teaching and learning.

Even though a researcher's 'world view' is not always stated explicitly, a good appreciation of the underlying assumptions of the research evidence being evaluated would help to discern how the study being reported aligns with the reader's own beliefs. This is important because ultimately, it is the practitioner as reader who is expected to gain some knowledge from the research evidence and be able to apply such knowledge to their practice.

Step 2: Identify the research questions

The introduction of a paper usually provides useful background information and context, and typically outlines the aims and objectives of the study. This should include the study's research question(s) or, in the case of experimental designs, research hypotheses. These can be powerful guides for teachers as critical practitioners because they provide an indication of whether the investigation and the associated findings are of immediate relevance to their practice. The research question(s) or hypotheses should give the reader a clue as to whether there is any relation between the study and their own challenges (or questions) which had prompted them to seek out further evidence.

Step 3: Review the research design and methodology

Research design, including the methodological framework, is another consideration in the appraisal process. Policymakers favour evidence drawn from RCTs and systematic reviews as they aim to establish cause and effect and the extent to which the evidence might be generalisable and scalable to a broad range of contexts. There is a debate to be had about the transferability of such designs from medicine to education, which is explored beyond this book (eg Philpott and Poultney, 2018). Others (eg Davies and Tedder, 2003; Flyvbjerg, 2001; Sfard, 1998) argue that case studies are the best way of studying relational complexity, such as the concept of learning, because they provide accounts that focus on the practices or activities through which people participate. This partly explains the prevalence of small-scale research, often case studies, in academic (and indeed practitioner) research. Conversely, this can be accused of not being scalable because the researchers sought to investigate people's attitudes, views and perceptions about a specified problem in a specific context.

What is important is to look at the rigour of the design and how it has been utilised in the context of a study and look for connections with the reader's own situation and interests. The more transparent a paper is about its methods, the more the reader can decide not only on its applicability but also on its quality – how credible, dependable and trustworthy it appears to them.

Step 4: Examine the discussion of findings and conclusion

When reviewing the presentation of findings, discussion and conclusion, it is important to consider whether the results are discussed in relation to similar (previous) studies. Issues raised with the interpretation of the research findings include:

- conclusions that are not supported by the results;

- inconsistences that have not been explained;

- exaggerations of the importance of the findings;

- inadequate discussion and interpretation of the data.

So, while the intention is not to disregard other people's academic endeavour, it is valid to question whether the data presented by the authors supports the conclusions being made. Equally it is important to examine any implicit or hidden assumptions that the authors may have used when interpreting their data because that can steer the discussion in a particular direction, which may influence the conclusions. Other points worth considering include any financial, ethical or other conflicts of interest associated with the study, its authors and sponsors.

Step 5: So, what?

From a practical perspective, a reader should move beyond the text of a research paper and talk to others, colleagues and peers about it. Because beyond this appraisal process is the important question: how can practitioners apply the 'learning' from research evidence to their practice?

As a professional, learning from reading and experiences are core aspects of personal and professional development. There are instances where a practitioner's response to specific tasks, activities, and duties challenge their values, perceptions, assumptions and interpretations of the world. Sometimes contradictions emerge between what has been read, and how this translates into practice. However, viewing these contradictions as an opportunity to learn enables a practitioner to turn them into a positive experience. A good way of dealing with this is through discussing the issue with colleagues at work, peers and friends who may be interested to test out the new understandings. The next section therefore explores some ideas about how social networking can support teacher professional development

7.6 Social networking and social media for teachers' professional learning and development

As discussed in Chapter 2, in education, the term 'networking' has been widely used in the change and school reform discourses and often promoted as a successful approach to school improvement (McCormick et al, 2010; Katz and Earl, 2010; Katz et al, 2009).

Building and/or extending networks

Network connections and relationships offer teachers the opportunity to access a range of formal and informal learning and development opportunities that are often not available within their schools. In the UK, TeachMeet is a good example of how educators network to share good practice. TeachMeets offer teachers the space to share practical innovations and personal insights in teaching (Walsh et al, 2011). In recent years these have grown in popularity and have been integrated into professional conferences, led by practitioners for practitioners.

The concept has grown beyond the UK with events now available in parts of North America. An even more recent phenomenon, being advertised through Twitter in the UK, is #BrewEd, in which teachers meet to discuss pedagogy over a drink in informal settings such as cafes or public houses (Egan-Simon and Finch, 2018).

Another example of educational networking and collaboration between and among people, schools and their communities, is ResearchED. This is a UK grass-roots, teacher-led organisation started in 2013 by Tom Bennett and colleagues. It aims to promote research into 'what works' and most importantly bring people together in social spaces (physical and virtual) for debate and dialogue. Similarly in North America the EdCAN Network has connected thousands of Canadian K-12 educators, researchers and partner groups. Social and professional networking in education continues to grow due to the potential benefits to participants such as:

- meeting like-minded people;

- sharing of ideas;

- connecting to other educational settings;

- professional development.

Strengthening research brokering through social media

The social media explosion in recent years has opened up opportunities to extend professional networking beyond physical 'meet ups' such as TeachMeets. The virtual environments created by social media platforms have helped overcome some of the challenges associated with face-to-face networking events. Through social media platforms such as Twitter, Facebook, LinkedIn, and more recently WhatsApp (for example Cansoy, 2017; Liana and Ngeze, 2015), teachers and, more broadly, educators can connect and follow each other's work without physical interaction.

Tweet chats have grown in popularity in recent years as a way of teacher collaboration which provide a virtual space for conversations about teaching and learning using Twitter (Britt and Paulus, 2016; Langhorst, 2015). The #Edchat Twitter hash tag facilitates such virtual conversations, #Edchat conversations are organised on specific days, with participants contributing to the discussions by adding #Edchat to their tweets. The potential of these well-organised social media events in generating practical evidence of what works should not be underestimated. Rather it should be harnessed in support of teacher professional learning and development (Emke, 2019).

7.7 Case studies

A model of a contemporary space in which teachers are both consumers and producers of evidence

CollectivED was set up in 2017 as a 'hub' for mentoring and coaching at the Carnegie School of Education at Leeds Beckett University. Its aim is to support professionals and researchers in a shared endeavour of enabling professional practice and learning with the potential to be transformative. This recognises teachers as both consumers and producers of research. It invites teachers and school leaders with a broad audience in mind to author: working papers (including summaries of empirical research), case studies, action research, practice-insight working papers and think-pieces. Teachers who engage in CollectivED programmes for mentoring and coaching are also encouraged to write reflective or enquiry-based papers. In addition, CollectivED hosts public events which provide opportunities for teachers and school leaders, and those working to support educational development (including researchers, consultants and teacher educators), to share practice and research evidence and enter into robust discussion. While CollectivED is relatively new this offers an innovative space in which teachers play key roles in creating, contributing and communicating knowledge through building new connections and collaborations.

Case study 2

Evidence-in-practice in action

Angel-Marie has been at Hibiscus School for over a decade and contributed immensely to the success of the pupils and school. As part of the school's efforts towards *evidence-in-practice* (E-IP), Angel-Marie took on coaching to support newly qualified teachers in their first year of teaching practice. Angel-Marie devised a scheme to collate and critically review evidence to help make an informed judgement about what could be included or excluded in her new induction programme.

As a starting point, Angel-Marie sought to investigate how the NQT induction programme in her school could be enhanced with the aim of implementing a programme that meets the needs and interests of NQTs. She approached this activity by focusing on challenges faced by NQTs, how they make sense of these (individually and collectively), and what strategies they adopted to meditate these challenges. To do this Angel-Marie studied three out of the six NQTs in her school for two terms and gathered detailed evidence about their experiences to facilitate the understanding of the complexities of their perspectives and activities, including how these change over time.

Angel-Marie's approach to evidence gathering is one that recognises the importance of context and the practitioner voice. Building on what is written about induction (within research evidence), she sets out to find out the situation in her own school which she then compared/contrasted with evidence generated elsewhere in published work. It is this contextual, close-to-practice enquiry process which can so powerfully drive school-level change.

7.8 Summary

Teachers can draw on the body of published evidence already produced and available, as long as they can gain access to, and critically evaluate, it and see how the findings might offer useful insights for their practice. This sees teachers as needing the skills to consume as well as produce evidence. This chapter has provided some such advice, although partnership-working, including master's study, will provide more bespoke CPD. At the end of each chapter this book has guided readers towards resources available through open access, rather than requiring journal subscription. A fuller reference list at the end of this book provides a wider evidence base to explore for those who have access.

Questions for enquiry within your own school

- What access is there to published research for staff in your setting? For example is there a CPD library or any online subscriptions?

- To what extent do those in your setting have personal access to published research, for example through professional associations, social media activity or while undertaking accredited study? If you can't answer this question, would it be useful to audit such access?

- Are there opportunities to discuss evidence produced beyond your setting, for example in leadership meetings, working groups or enquiry groups?

- Do staff feel empowered and confident to critically read and evaluate published research in ways which allow it to inform their thinking and potentially therefore also their practice? If you can't answer this question, would it be useful to audit staff attitudes and skills?

- Is supporting staff use of published research a potential priority area which could be incorporated into CPD structures and opportunities for training? If there are enthusiasts identified from answering the previous questions, might they be motivated to be involved in any such training or take a research leadership role such as running a reading group?

The following self-assessment toolkit developed by Stoll et al (2018) is recommended, because it supports teachers in assessing:

- their level of awareness about evidence-informed practice;

  the extent to which they engage with the ideas;

- the degree to which research evidence is actively used to investigate and change practice.

The toolkit is available at: https://chartered.college/wp-content/uploads/2018/01/Evidence-informed-teaching-self-assessment-tool-for-teachers.pdf

Useful websites

Academia: www.academia.edu

British Educational Research Association (BERA) Blog: www.bera.ac.uk/blog

CollectivED: www.leedsbeckett.ac.uk/carnegie-school-of-education/research/collectivED

EdCAN Network: www.edcan.ca

ResearchED: https://researched.org.uk/

ResearchGate: www.researchgate.net

Chapter 8
Conclusions and take-aways

Alison Fox

8.1 Chapter overview

This chapter will outline:

8.2   the case for the value of PLCs and teacher enquiry;

8.3   guidance on alternative options for teacher collaboration and enquiry;

8.4   evidence-based advice for the leadership of collective teacher enquiry;

8.5   evidence-based advice for engagement with collective teacher enquiry;

8.6   guidance on monitoring and evaluating impact of enquiry in your setting.

8.2 The case for PLCs and collaborative teacher enquiry

This book has offered a critically reflective review of the evidence base which can inform advice about collaborative teacher enquiry for school improvement. Evidence and counter-evidence reveal key challenges for envisioning and practising community-building and supporting teacher enquiry. As well as looking at the practical activities involved, underlying principles which explain the aspirations and behaviours have been identified. This has identified the importance of having a contextual understanding of national and local, including internal institutional, constraints to appreciate how these can affect the realisation of visions for and directions of such activities. An understanding of the geography and history of research into various forms of teacher assemblage (team, community, partnership and network) associated with teacher enquiry has been brought together to inform decision-making and practical actions.

Selected macro- and meso-evidence (using the typology of scales of evidence in Chapter 7) is collated for four key claims made about teacher collaborative enquiry:

1.   teacher collaborative enquiry is worthwhile;

2.   the main challenges are constraints on leader agency;

3.   a significant challenge is a lack of adequate resourcing;

4. inertia should not be overlooked as a potential hurdle to instigating teacher collaborative enquiry.

Micro-evidence, ie from smaller-scale studies, has been indicated within each of the chapters as points were made.

Claim 1: Teacher collaborative enquiry is worthwhile

On balance, evidence in this book supports the value of teachers asking questions of their practice and practice settings to collectively, with one another and critical friends such as from universities, gathering evidence in ways which help address these questions and so informing decisions for future practice. The UK policy environment began to capture aspirations for evidence-based teaching, for example from DfE-commissioned reports (Goldacre, 2013a), reviews (The Carter Review, DfE, 2015) and, seminally, the Education White Paper *Educational Excellence Everywhere* (DfE, 2016a). This built on discourse about educational improvement by policymakers, researchers and teacher educators which promoted close-to-practice enquiry as a mechanism for school and indeed education system improvement (Hargreaves, D, 2003, 2010, 2011). The White Paper launched a new *Standard for Teachers' Professional Development* (DfE, 2016b) which is worth reporting in some detail here (see Table 8a) to show the alignment with the body of evidence presented in this book.

Table 8a UK advice for teachers' professional development (DfE, 2016b, p 1)

Effective teacher professional development is a partnership between:
• Headteachers and other members of the leadership team; • Teachers; and • Providers of professional development expertise, training or consultancy.
In order for this partnership to be successful:
1. Professional development should have a focus on improving and evaluating pupil outcomes. 2. Professional development should be underpinned by robust evidence and expertise. 3. Professional development should include collaboration and expert challenge. 4. Professional development programmes should be sustained over time. And all this is underpinned by, and requires that: 5. Professional development must be prioritised by school leadership.

The standard refers to professional development as involving teachers in **partnership** with others, needing to be **evidence**-based, including **collaboration**, in **sustained** ways and led by **school leadership**.

The following tables (8b–8e) summarise the key evidence and take-away advice for each of the claims.

Table 8b Evidence supporting teacher collaborative enquiry as worthwhile

	Key evidence	Take-away
Macro-evidence	Levine (2010)	Note alternative conceptualisations of teacher collaborative enquiry which prioritise different purposes.
	Sahlberg (2010)	Recognise that teacher expectations of and capacity for collaborative enquiry need to be systematically built into an educational system
	Stenhouse (1968, 1975, 1981, 1983) and Elliott (1980, 1999, 2004); Harris and Jones (2017)	Value practitioner enquiry as a valid source of evidence to inform teaching and learning and hence school improvement.
	Hargreaves, D (2011); Day and Sachs (2004)	Need to develop agreed shared values and aspirations empowering all involved.
	Philpott and Poultney (2018); Poultney (2017)	Need the profession to have a shared commitment to self-renewal to be called a profession.
	Hargreaves, D (2003); McLaughlin et al (2006, 2007); Muijs et al (2010)	Need teacher professional development to be based itself on a critical review of available evidence.
	Stoll (2010); Stoll and Louis (2007); Stoll et al (2006, 2012a, 2012b, 2018); Bolam et al (2005)	See school-to-school networking for enquiry as the way forward for schools to collaborate rather than compete.

	Key evidence	Take-away
		Note that PLCs offer schools the way to think about collaborative enquiry within but especially beyond their physical borders.
Meso-evidence	DfE (2016b)	Work within explicit UK-wide expectation for collaborative and sustained teacher development.
	Armstrong (2015); Lindsay et al (2007); Chapman et al (2016)	Need leaders to build on past collaborations with good relationships, developing a culture of collegiality, trust and using effective communications.
	Nelson et al (2015a, 2015b); Maxwell et al (2015)	Recognise that over time social, cultural and decisional capital develops, enhancing inclusion and extending beyond the school community. Evidence of positive impact on disadvantaged student performance.
		Build trust and shared agendas which can contribute to building on this.
		Increase capacity of all concerned to be critical of assumptions and norms.
	Goodnough (2011)	Note the likely motivational and developmental benefits for staff involved.
		Note that staff turnover need not necessarily be a challenge.
	Cain (2015); Cain et al (2016)	Note the role for teachers in mobilising and hence acting on published educational research knowledge.

Claim 2: The main challenge to teacher collaborative enquiry is constraints on leader agency

Table 8c Evidence about the challenges for leadership of teacher collaborative enquiry

	Key evidence	Take-away
Macro-evidence	DuFour and Eaker (1998)	Need to balance focus on teacher learning to counter international focus on pupil performance.
	Wenger et al (2002); Wenger- Trayner et al (2015)	Need to value outward looking dimension to community-building.
	Hargreaves, A (1994, 1997, 2007); McGregor (2004)	Need to overcome accountability pressures recognising the Balkanisation of schools.
	Bottery (2003)	Need to see the value of enquiry and of collaboration, to be motivated to create the cultures and structures, times and spaces for teachers to meet.
Meso-evidence		Need to be aware of and compensate for:
	Chapman et al (2009) Woods et al (2006) Lindsay et al (2007) Haynes and Lynch (2013) Opfer and Pedder (2011a)	the challenges of working beyond the home school environment in a competitive accountability culture;
		perceived power imbalances between schools;
		external drivers to collaborate are not sufficient.
		Best to be driven by internal motivations.

	Key evidence	Take-away
	Woods et al (2006)	In low performing schools the high levels of performance management and narrower professional learning opportunities are counterproductive to school improvement.

High staff turnover, while a threat, is not necessarily so if vision and structures for sustainability are in place. |

Claim 3: A significant challenge to teacher collaborative enquiry is a lack of adequate resourcing

Table 8d Evidence about the challenges of under-resourcing for effective teacher collaborative enquiry

	Key evidence	Take-away
Meso-evidence	Lindsay et al (2007)

Woods et al (2006)

Bloom (2016)

See et al (2016) | A lack of confidence in the sustainability of funding constrains leadership commitment.

Concentrated funding on projects and looking for opportunities to use this for leverage and synergy with other projects are effective strategies.

Time is the most constraining resource, yet vital for collaboration and engagement with enquiry. Strategies to overcome this are needed in negotiation with staff involved.

Need for leadership support, which requires clearer guidance, professional development and modelling of strategies suggested. |

Claim 4: Inertia should not be overlooked as a potential hurdle to instigating teacher collaborative enquiry

Table 8e Evidence about the challenges of inertia in school settings for effective teacher collaborative enquiry

	Key evidence	Take-away
Macro-evidence	Little (1990, 2005) Hargreaves, A (1994, 1997, 2007)	Recognise the persistence of inward-looking teaching in isolation, whether in individual classrooms or siloed ways of working within schools. Also note the dangers of groupthink and the need to look externally, developing outward-looking behaviours.
	Achinstein (2002); de Lima (2001, 2007)	Note that just putting teachers together is insufficient as need to recognise the influence of micropolitics. Look beyond social relationships to developing critical friendships and complementary assemblages of teachers.
Meso-evidence	Carmichael et al (2006); Young (2006)	Value weak links or 'loose coupling', noting the role of brokers to bridge to other sources of support and the role of research champions to mobilise energy and enthusiasm in schools.
	Krammer et al (2018)	Recognise differences in teacher perception of shared responsibility and enjoyment of engaging in collaborative enquiry as the starting point for collaboration.

8.3 Practical advice when selecting forms of collaborative enquiry

In terms of the different forms of collaborative enquiry introduced in Chapter 2 and explored in the subsequent chapters Table 8f offers a comparison to guide thinking about which form of enquiry to be involved in or to initiate.

Table 8f A comparison of forms of collaborative enquiry

Developing...	Useful when you...	Key actions are to...	Advantages are...	Things to consider are...
Teams or Knotworks	Want a task completing	Make clear expectations and ensure team feel can achieve these Schedule work Set monitoring points Offer support and/or training	Shares workload Empowers staff	Self-selecting teams not necessarily the most effective but most liked by teachers May want to select team members for particular and comple-mentary skills
Communities (PLCs, CoPs or communities of enquiry)	Want to develop a sense of belonging for the benefit for practice	Ensure clear and agreed focus Provide mechanisms for participation which encourage sense of belonging Welcome newcomers actively	Can become self-sustaining with newcomers being included and developed by those committed to the activities	Need more support than just time and spaces to spend together Expect to be dynamic and be aware of the dangers of groupthink

Developing...	Useful when you...	Key actions are to...	Advantages are...	Things to consider are...
		Encourage connectivity beyond the community	Increases job satisfaction and motivation as reduce isolation	
Partnerships	Want to establish learning which draws from beyond organisation	Negotiate aims and aspired outcomes Explore together effective spaces, times and ways of working Self-evaluate progress against aims and aspired outcomes, including reviewing whether they are still valid	Draw on the strengths of different bodies of knowledge and ways of working for mutual benefit	The potential for power imbalances is important to reveal in order to plan to counter these
Networks	Want to draw on the increasing knowledge-base held across individuals and organisations locally, nationally and internationally	Recognise the existing social capital which individuals already hold Actively maintain relationships	Brings in new ideas, practices and ways of thinking Re-energises ways of working	Many parts of an individual's valued networks are personal

Developing...	Useful when you...	Key actions are to...	Advantages are...	Things to consider are...
		Consider social media as a vehicle for networking for professional learning	A wide range of individuals can bring value to collective work	Networking challenges the boundaries of work and life: a tension as well as an opportunity
		Identify which parts of networks could benefit particular activities and activate these		

8.4 Practical advice for the leadership of collaborative teacher enquiry

These take-aways for school leaders relate to both the vision and the practice of leadership needed to maximise the benefits of collaborative teacher enquiry for school improvement, These relate to cultivating the conditions for teacher agency and empowerment as part of this bigger endeavour.

David Hargreaves, in his development of advice for schools about becoming part of a self-sustaining school system, produced a maturity model with 12 strands needing leadership attention. This is a useful device for summarising the advice contained in this book (Table 8g).

Table 8g An interpretation of Hargreaves' (2012) maturity model for school improvement

The activities	Leadership considerations
The professional development dimension and its strands	
Joint practice development	JPD can be interpreted in many ways and is not a single approach. It cannot be achieved simply by expecting teachers to work with one another. JPD needs leadership support, including finding ways of showing it is valued.
Mentoring and coaching	More experienced members of professional communities can play a valuable role in supporting others in developing enquiries. These will need to be selected for their expertise and enthusiasm in enquiry.
Talent identification	Teachers hold interests, aspirations, social capital associated with their networks which are not always immediately evident in their day-to-day practice. Ways of finding out more about the talent held within the staff could form part of regular discussions with line managers.
Distributed staff information	Communication with staff will be vital to communicating the aspirations for, maintaining impetus for and disseminating the outcomes of enquiry.
The partnership competence dimension and its strands	
Fit governance	Equity is an important aspiration for the strategic governance of partnership-working, ensuring that any perceived power imbalances are worked towards being overcome. This might affect with whom partnerships are formed, should particularly affect the agenda setting and aspirations of the partnership and also be kept under review.
	Communities and networks are not usually characterised by such formal oversight, although can be contrived to an extent. In all situations, power imbalances should be recognised and self-evaluated as to the effect on these as constraining or affording enquiry.

The activities	Leadership considerations
High social capital	The collective networks from all with whom teachers work, if made explicit, offer a powerful resource for all. Processes to make explicit this access to knowledge is needed.
Collective moral purpose, or distributed system leadership	The vision should not be constrained to those setting up and leading any teams, partnerships or communities. Distributing leadership needs to empower teachers to realise their agency and encourage a sense of belonging, to develop their commitment to the collective purpose. How this is enacted will depend on how self-selected or contrived the assemblages are.
Evaluation and challenge	A clarity of purpose and agreed outcomes will enable success criteria to be articulated. This allows for both self-evaluation by those involved, for formative uses as the activity progresses, as well as summatively being able to report to those to whom the activity is accountable. If the criteria are agreed by those within the assemblage, external evaluators should be able to offer critical friend feedback on progress towards or achievement of outcomes. As activity is likely to be long-term and aiming at sustainability, milestones will need to be identified and timescales for reaching these negotiated.
The collaborative capital dimension and its strands	
Analytical investigation	Deciding on the focus for enquiry will depend on how ideas for what is worthwhile to study are prioritised. Greatest engagement with enquiry will arise when those involved have a stake in identifying its focus. Aligning interests with school or even wider Alliance/Cluster/Federation/Partnership agendas will require thoughtful leadership.

The activities	Leadership considerations
Disciplined innovation	Enquiry which is systematic needs staff training for them to be able to generate reliable evidence. Support for this can be gained from working in school–university partnerships and from individuals who are engaged in university-supported study. Schools can benefit from developing teachers as critical consumers of published research especially given the increasing access to this research.
Creative entrepreneurship	It is important to value teacher commitment to the profession and the ideas of all members in order to bring new ideas to the table. This should include drawing on the expertise of others beyond a school from networks and partnership-working.
Alliance architecture	Structures and spaces are needed as well as ways of working which support 'third space' collaboration across usual boundaries. New technologies can assist in this as explored and agreed by those involved. It should be recognised that social media participation often moves beyond the school work place and day encroaching into personal spaces and times, which it should not be assumed all teachers will be committed to.

In summary, the evidence for sustainable systems of collaborative enquiry that can accommodate staff turnover (Chapman et al, 2009), need leaders that are:

- outward-looking;
- forward thinking;
- open to collaboration as a means of improvement;
- committed to trust-building;
- good communicators;
- offer and seek out critical friendship.

8.5 Practical considerations for engagement with collective teacher enquiry

This book has presented a message to teachers which it is hoped will have shown the value of working with other teachers and professionals as a central right for teachers as professionals. The case studies and illustrations have been included as opportunities to hear about concrete experiences of collaborative teacher enquiry. Collaborative teacher enquiry has been presented as an agentic and empowering vision for re-invigorating the profession from a grassroots perspective, with teachers as activists collectively seeking to maximise educational provision for young people. It is hoped this has been shown to have the potential for remotivation at a time when practitioners are increasingly burdened by administrative tasks and the demands of accountability frameworks, with the benefits of increasing job satisfaction, well-being and therefore continued commitment to the profession.

As advocated in Chapter 2 at a school level, a means of acting on the advice in this book can be summarised in the form of a Strength–Weakness–Opportunities–Threats (SWOT) analysis for individual practitioners to identify their needs, actions and monitoring as part of continuous professional-development planning.

Table 8h A SWOT analysis to guide collaborative enquiry-readiness

Strengths – what interests, energies, network contacts, attitudes, skills do you bring to the enquiry?	**Weaknesses** – what are your personal concerns, skills for which you would want support? From whom could you get support?
Opportunities – what would you like to get involved with? Is there enquiry which already exists or you have heard about? Can you see a challenge which could be addressed by enquiry?	**Threats** – what do you think the biggest challenges will be and what can be done to overcome these? Who do you need help from to overcome these?

8.6 Monitoring and evaluating impact of enquiry in your setting

Questions for enquiry in your setting have been included in Chapter 1 (about initiating enquiry), Chapter 3 (to support partnership-working), Chapter 4 (to support collaborative enquiry) and Chapter 6 (when considering leading professional community-building) and key actions suggested in Chapter 2 (about different forms of enquiry), Chapter 5 (if adopting Lesson Study) and Chapter 7 (a five-stage process of advice in relation to critical reading). As a framework for reflecting on these chapter summaries and setting up an action, monitoring and evaluation plan, the following framework (Table 8i), suggests that actions relevant to your setting are mapped against five key aims for collaborative enquiry arising from this book.

Table 8i A framework for a collaborative teacher enquiry action, monitoring and evaluation plan

	Action	Monitoring	Success criteria	Evaluation
Aim 1: Identifying and motivating partners/ collaborators				
Aim 2: Agreeing outcomes				
Aim 3: Negotiating mutually convenient ways of working				
Aim 4: Drawing on external links				
Aim 5: Providing training				

Questions for enquiry in your own school

Before you start completing such an action plan, it would be worth reviewing the current situation, with colleagues in your setting; ideally those who will be or could be involved in and affected by the collaborative work. These questions can be used to guide the completion of the above framework.

- Where are you starting from?

- What do you want to achieve?

- How do you feel collaborative enquiry can help with these intended outcomes?

- Which skills and resources are needed?

- Which of these skills and resources are already available and which need to be sourced?

- How will you know that you have achieved your intended outcomes?

It is worth referring back to the advice given by the IASCE (The International Association for the Study of Cooperation in Education) in Chapter 1 about the principles which should underpin the action planning process; a critical, flexible and persistent approach will be needed to realise the potential of teacher collaboration (Baloche and Brody, 2017).

8.7 Summary

This book has drawn together evidence about collaborative teacher enquiry. A set of key principles were drawn from 40 years of enquiry into teacher co-operation across eight countries by the International Association for the Study of Cooperation in Education (IASCE) (Baloche and Brody, 2017, p 281) to:

(a) examine beliefs;

(b) identify problems;

(c) utilise research as a foundation for innovation;

(d) understand context and thinking incrementally;

(e) build communities for enquiry, experimentation, and support;

(f) be willing to fail;

(g) recognise when something does not work.

These principles have been reflected in the advice for practice in each chapter. However, the IASCE advocate persistence if the potential of teacher collaboration is to be realised, beyond buy-in to the principles and understanding of the challenges (Baloche and Brody, 2017).

Useful websites

The Education Endowment Foundation: https://educationendowmentfoundation.org.uk/evidence-summaries/teaching-learning-toolkit

The Chartered College of Teaching: https://chartered.college

The Sutton Trust: www.suttontrust.com

The EPPI-Centre: http://eppi.ioe.ac.uk/cms

The Teacher Development Trust: https://tdtrust.org

The Research Schools Network: https://researchschool.org.uk

The Teacher Education Advancement Network journal: www.cumbria.ac.uk/research/enterprise/tean/tean-journal

Afterword: a note about terminology

The language surrounding evidence-based practice has shifted in the time that this book series has been developed. When the series was first launched there was felt to be a need for publications which spoke up for those in the education profession who were developing practice supported by firm foundations of evidence. A need for teachers to be supported in critically evaluating this evidence led to this Critical Publishing book series entitled *Evidence-based Teaching for Enquiring Teachers*. The idea for the book series came at a time when an increasing volume of advice was being offered to schools, often with a commercial bias, which was not necessarily easily traceable to its origins in sound evidence.

As evidence-based practice became part of the language about teacher professionalism and school improvement it also became open to critique (see for example Connolly, 2018; Gale, 2018; Gorard et al, 2017). Commentators emphasised the origins of this phrasing in medical fields and the dangers of appropriating this model in which only certain types of study were considered as robust and reliable enough to provide evidence on which to base practice decisions (eg Biesta, 2007; Wrigley, 2018). This sees large-scale, randomised trials as the 'gold standard'. To ensure that the wider range of forms of evidence on which practitioners can and should base their pedagogical, curricular and assessment practices, are recognised academics proposed that the terminology 'evidence-informed practice' should be used. Interestingly those in the medical and health fields have in parallel moved to make a similar case (eg Rycroft-Malone, 2008; Nevo and Slonim-Nevo, 2011; Woodbury and Kuhnke, 2014).

This book series has never been based on advocating a 'what works' approach to evidence (Biesta, 2007). It has instead contributed to the debate of critically engaging with a wide range of forms of evidence, including that generated by practitioners themselves. This book, *Professional Learning Communities and Teacher Enquiry*, takes on this particular aspect of evidence-building while setting such activity within the wider political context outlined in this afterword, in order to support awareness-raising of the issues and opportunities of basing practice development on evidence.

References

Achinstein, B (2002) Conflict Amid Community: The Micropolitics of Teacher Collaboration. *Teachers College Record,* 104(3): 421–45.

Akiba, M and Wilkinson, B (2016) Adopting an International Innovation for Teacher Professional Development. *Journal of Teacher Education,* 67(1): 74–93.

Amin, A and Roberts, J (2008) Knowing in Action: Beyond Communities of Practice. *Research Policy,* 37(2): 353–69.

Anderson, G L, Herr, K and Nihlen, A S (2007) *Studying Your Own School: An Educator's Guide to Practitioner Action Research.* Thousand Oaks, CA: Corwin Press.

Armstrong, P (2015) *Effective School Partnerships and Collaboration for School Improvement: A Review of the Evidence: Research Report DFE-RR466.* London: Department for Education. [online] Available at: https://assets. publishing.service.gov.uk/government/uploads/system/uploads/attachment_ data/file/467855/DFE-RR466_-_School_improvement_effective_school_ partnerships.pdf (accessed 30 July 2019).

Arthur, L, Marland, H, Pill, A and Rea, T (2006) Postgraduate Professional Development for Teachers: Motivational and Inhibiting Factors Affecting the Completion of Awards. *Journal of In-Service Education,* 32(2): 201–19.

Bain, Y, Bruce, J and Weir, D (2017) Changing the Landscape of School–University Partnership in Northern Scotland. *Professional Development in Education,* 43(4): 537–55.

Baker-Doyle, K (2011) *The Networked Teacher: How New Teachers Build Social Networks for Professional Support.* New York: Teachers Hall Press.

Baker-Doyle, K and Yoon, S (2011) In Search of Practitioner-based Social Capital: a Social Network Analysis Tool for Understanding and Facilitating Teacher Collaboration in a US-based STEM Professional Development Program. *Professional Development in Education,* 37(1): 75–93.

Ball, S J (2012) *The Micro-Politics of the School: Towards a Theory of School Organization.* London: Routledge.

Baloche, L and Brody, C M (2017) Cooperative Learning: Exploring Challenges, Crafting Innovations. *Journal of Education for Teaching: International Research and Pedagogy, Special Issue: Cooperative Learning: Exploring Challenges, Crafting Innovations,* 43(3): 274–83.

Barth, R S (1984) The Principalship. *Educational Leadership*, 42(2): 93.

Beckett, L (2016) *Teachers and Academic Partners in Urban Schools: Threats to Professional Practice*. London and New York: Routledge.

Beijaard, D, Meijer, P C and Verloop, N (2004) Reconsidering Research on Teachers' Professional Identity. *Teaching and Teacher Education*, 20(2): 107–28.

Biesta, G (2007) Why 'What Works' Won't Work: Evidence-based Practice and the Democratic Deficit in Educational Research. *Educational theory*, 57(1): 1–22.

Biesta, G (2015) On the Two Cultures of Educational Research, and How We Might Move Ahead: Reconsidering the Ontology, Axiology and Praxeology of Education. *European Educational Research Journal*, 14: 11–22.

Bloom, A (2016) Teachers Do Not Have Time to Learn about Research Evidence, Studies Find, *Times Educational Supplement*, 20 May 2016. [online] Available at: www.tes.com/news/teachers-do-not-have-time-learn-about-research-evidence-studies-find (accessed 30 July 2019).

Bolam, R, McMahon, A, Stoll, L, Thomas, S and Wallace, M (2005) *Creating and Sustaining Effective Professional Learning Communities* (Research Report RR637). London: Department for Education and Skills. [online] Available at: https://dera.ioe.ac.uk/5622/1/RR637.pdf (accessed 30 July 2019).

Borg, S (2006) Conditions for Teacher Research. *English Teaching Forum*, 44(4): 22–7. Washington: US Department of State. Bureau of Educational and Cultural Affairs, Office of English Language Programs.

Borg, S and Sanchez, H (eds) (2015) *International Perspectives on Teacher Research*. London: Palgrave Macmillan.

Bosworth, A G and Murphy, M P and Facebook Inc, (2015) *Identify Experts and Influencers in a Social Network*. U.S. Patent 8,954,503. [online] Available at: https://patentimages.storage.googleapis.com/23/f0/2c/ef158d38b8ec2a/US8954503.pdf (accessed 30 July 2019).

Bottery, M (2003) The Leadership of Learning Communities in a Culture of Unhappiness. *School Leadership and Management*, 23(2): 187–207.

Brazdau, O (2016) *Consciousness Quotient Institute*. [online] Available at: www.consciousness-quotient.com (accessed 30 July 2019).

Breault, D (2013) The Challenges of Scaling-up and Sustaining Professional Development School Partnerships. *Teaching and Teacher Education*, 36: 92–100.

Brehm, J and Rahn, W (1997) Individual-Level Evidence for the Causes and Consequences of Social Capital. *American Journal of Political Science*, 41(3): 999–1023.

British Educational Research Association–Royal Society for the Encouragement of the Arts, Manufacturing and Commerce (BERA–RSA) (2014) *Research and the Teaching Profession: Building the Capacity for a Self-improving Education System: Final Report of the BERA-RSA Inquiry into the Role of Research in Teacher Education.* London: BERA. [online] Available at: www.bera.ac.uk/wp-content/uploads/2013/12/BERA-RSA-Research-Teaching-Profession-FULL-REPORT-for-web.pdf?noredirect=1 (accessed 30 July 2019).

Britt, V G and Paulus, T (2016) Beyond the Four Walls of My Building: A Case Study of #Edchat as a Community of Practice. *American Journal of Distance Education,* 30(1): 48–59.

Broadhead, P (2010) 'Insiders' and 'Outsiders' Researching Together to Create New Understandings and to Shape Policy and Practice: Is It All Possible? In Campbell, A and Groundwater-Smith, S (eds) *Connecting Inquiry and Professional Learning in Education: International Perspectives and Practical Solutions.* London and New York: Routledge.

Brown, C (2013) *Making Evidence Matter: A New Perspective for Evidence-informed Policy Making in Education.* London: Institute of Education, University of London.

Brown, C and Bennett, T (2015) *Leading the Use of Research and Evidence in Schools.* London: IOE Press.

Brown, C, Schildkamp, K and Hubers, M D (2017) Combining the Best of Two Worlds: A Conceptual Proposal for Evidence-informed School Improvement. *Educational Research,* 59(2): 154–72.

Brundrett, M (1998) What Lies Behind Collegiality, Legitimation or Control? An Analysis of the Purported Benefits of Collegial Management in Education. *Educational Management, Administration and Leadership,* 26(3): 305–16.

Bruner, J S (1961). The Act of Discovery. *Harvard Educational Review,* 31(1): 21–32.

Butler, D L, Schnellert, L and Higginson, S K (2008) Co-Constructors of Data, Co-Constructors of Meaning: Teacher Professional Development in an Age of Accountability. *Teaching and Teacher Education,* 24(3): 725–50.

Cain, T (2015) Teachers' Engagement with Research Texts: Beyond Instrumental, Conceptual or Strategic Use. *Journal of Education for Teaching,* 41: 478–92.

Cain, T (2017) Denial, Opposition, Rejection or Dissent: Why Do Teachers Contest Research Evidence? *Research Papers in Education,* 32(5): 611–25.

Cain, T, Wieser, C and Livingston, K (2016) Mobilising Research Knowledge for Teaching and Teacher Education. *European Journal of Teacher Education,* 39(5): 529–33.

Cajkler, W and Wood, P (2016) Mentors and Student-Teachers 'Lesson Studying' in Initial Teacher Education. *International Journal for Lesson and Learning Studies*, 5(2): 1–18.

Cajkler, W, Wood P, Norton J and Pedder, D (2013) Lesson Study: Towards a Collaborative Approach to Learning in Initial Teacher Education? *Cambridge Journal of Education*, 43(4): 537–54.

Cansoy, R (2017) Teachers' Professional Development: The Case of WhatsApp. *Journal of Education and Learning*, 6(4): 285–93.

Carmichael, P (2011) *Networking Research: New Directions in Educational Inquiry*. London: Continuum.

Carmichael, P, Fox, A, McCormick, R, Procter, R and Honour, L (2006) Teachers' Networks In and Out of School. *Research Papers in Education*, 21(2): 217–34.

Carnegie Foundation (2019) *About Us*. New York: Carnegie Foundation for the Advancement of Teaching. [online] Available at: www.carnegiefoundation.org/about-us/foundation-history (accessed 30 July 2019).

Carnegie Task Force on Teaching as a Profession (1986) *A Nation Prepared: Teachers For The 21st Century*. New York: Carnegie Foundation.

Castells, M (2000) *The Rise of the Network Society. Volume I. The Information Age: Economy, Society and Culture*, 2nd edn. Oxford: Blackwell.

Chapman, C (2009) Towards a Framework for School-to-school Networking in Challenging Circumstances. *Educational Research*, 50(4): 403–20.

Chapman, C, Chestnutt, H, Friel, N, Hall, S and Lowden, K (2016) Professional Capital and Collaborative Inquiry Networks for Educational Equity and Improvement? *Journal of Professional Capital and Community*, 1(3): 178–97.

Chapman, C, Muijs, M, Sammons, P, Armstrong, P and Collins, A (2009) *The Impact of Federations on Student Outcomes*. A Report prepared for the National College of Leadership for Schools and Children's Services. Nottingham: National College for School Leadership.

Church, M, Bitel, M, Armstrong, K, Fernando, P, Gould, H, Joss, S, Marwaha-Diedrich, M, Laura de la Torre, A and Vouhé, C (2002) *Participation, Relationships and Dynamic Change: New Thinking On Evaluating The Work Of International Networks*, Working Paper No. 12. London: Development Planning Unit ISSN 1474–3280. [online] Available at: www.eldis.org/document/A14193 (accessed 30 July 2019).

Churches, R (2016) *Closing the Gap: Test and Learn Research Report*. DFE-RR500b. London: HMSO.

Clegg, S (2005) Evidence-based Practice in Educational Research: A Critical Realist Critique of Systematic Review. *British Journal of Sociology of Education*, 26(3): 415–28.

Clement, J (2013) Managing Mandated Educational Change. *School Leadership and Management*, 34(1): 39–51.

Cochran-Smith, M and Lytle, S L (1993) *Inside Out: Teacher Research and Knowledge*. New York: Teachers College Press.

Cochran-Smith, M and Lytle, S L (1999) The Teacher Research Movement: A Decade Later. *Educational Researcher*, 28(7): 15–25.

Cochran-Smith, M and Lytle, S L (2009) *Enquiry as Stance: Practitioner Research for the Next Generation*. New York: Teachers College Press.

Coldwell, M, Greany, T, Higgins, S, Brown, C, Maxwell, B, Stiell, B, Stoll, L, Willis, B and Burns, H (2017) *Evidence-informed Teaching: An Evaluation of Progress in England*. Research Report, July 2017. London: Department for Education. [online] Available at: www.gov.uk/government/uploads/system/uploads/attachment_data/file/625007/Evidence-informed_teaching_-_an_evaluation_of_progress_in_England.pdf (accessed 30 July 2019).

Collaborative Action Research Network-Action Learning: Action Research Association (CARN-ALARA) (2019) About us. [online] Available at: https://carn-alara2019.org/about-carn (accessed 30 July 2019).

Collins English Dictionary (2018) London: HarperCollins Publications. [online] Available at: www.collinsdictionary.com/dictionary/english/community (accessed 30 July 2019).

Connolly, P (2018) The Future Promise of RCTs in Education: Some Reflections on Closing the Gap Project. In Childs, A and Menter, I (eds) *Mobilising Teacher Researchers: Challenging Educational Inequality*. London and New York: Routledge.

Cooper, A, Klinger, A D and McAdie, P (2017) What do Teachers Need? An Exploration of Evidence-informed Practice for Classroom Assessment in Ontario. *Educational Research*, 59(2): 190–208.

Cordingley, P (2008) Research and Evidence-informed Practice: Focusing on Practice and Practitioners. *Cambridge Journal of Education*, 38(1): 37–52.

Cornelissen, J, Delios, A and Floyd, S W (2006) Limits to Communities of Practice. *Journal of Management Studies*, 43(3): 621–22.

Crozier, G and Davies, J (2013) Hard to Reach Parents or Hard to Reach Schools? A Discussion of Home–School Relations, with Particular Reference to Bangladeshi and Pakistani parents. *British Educational Research Journal*, 33(3): 295–313.

Curry, M W (2008) Critical Friends Groups: The Possibilities and Limitations Embedded in Teacher Professional Communities Aimed at Instructional Improvement and School Reform. *Teachers College Record*, 114(4): 733–74.

Datnow, A (2011) Collaboration and Contrived Collegiality: Revisiting Hargreaves in the Age of Accountability. *Journal of Educational Change*, 12(2): 147–58.

Davies, J and Tedder, M (2003) Becoming Vocational: Insights from Two Vocational Courses in a Further Educational College. *Journal of Vocational Education and Training*, 55(4): 517–39.

Day, C (2017) *Teachers' Worlds and Work: Understanding Complexity, Building Quality.* London and New York: Routledge.

Day, C and Sachs, J (2004) Professionalism, Performativity and Empowerment: Discourses in the Politics, Policies and Purposes of Continuing Professional Development. In Day, C and Sachs, J (eds) *International Handbook on the Continuing Professional Development of Teachers* (pp 1–32). Maidenhead: Open University Press.

de Carvalho, M E (2000) *Rethinking Family-School Relations: A Critique of Parental Involvement in Schooling.* London: Routledge.

de Lima, J Á (2001) Forgetting about Friendship: Using Conflict in Teacher Communities as a Catalyst for School Change. *Journal of Educational Change*, 2: 97.

de Lima, J Á (2007) Teachers' Professional Development in Departmentalised, Loosely Coupled Organisations: Lessons for School Improvement From a Case Study of Two Curriculum Departments. *School Effectiveness and School Improvement: An International Journal of Research, Policy and Practice*, 18(3): 271–303.

DeLuca, C, Bolden, B and Chan, J (2017) Systemic Professional Learning Through Collaborative Enquiry: Examining Teachers' Perspectives. *Teaching and Teacher Education*, 67(1): 67–78.

Department for Education (2015) *Carter Review of Initial Teacher Training.* Report, DFE-00036-2015. London: HMSO. [online] Available at: www.gov.uk/government/publications/carter-review-of-initial-teacher-training (accessed 30 July 2019).

Department for Education (2016a) *Educational Excellence Everywhere: A White Paper Setting Out Our Vision for Schools in England*. London: HMSO. [online] Available at: www.gov.uk/government/publications/educational-excellence-everywhere (accessed 30 July 2019).

Department for Education (2016b) *Standard for Teachers' Professional Development*, Report, 160712. London: HMSO. [online] Available at: https://assets.publishing.service.gov.uk/government/uploads/system/uploads/attachment_data/file/537030/160712_-_PD_standard.pdf (accessed 30 July 2019).

Department for Education (2019) *Early Career Framework*. DFE-00015-2019. London: HMSO. [online] Available at: https://assets.publishing.service.gov.uk/government/uploads/system/uploads/attachment_data/file/773705/Early-Career_Framework.pdf (accessed 30 July 2019).

Dewey, J (1933) *How We Think: A Restatement of the Relation of Reflective Thinking to the Educative Process*. Boston, MA: DC Heath.

Dionne, S D, Yammarino, F J, Atwater, L E and Spangler, W D (2004) Transformational Leadership and Team Performance. *Journal of Organizational Change Management*, 17(2): 177–93.

Dron, J and Anderson, T (2014a) *Teaching Crowds – Learning and Social Media*. Edmonton: AU Press.

Dron, J and Anderson, T (2014b) On the Design of Social Media for Learning. *Social Sciences*, 3(3): 378–93.

Dudley, P (2011) Lesson Study Development in England: From School Networks to National Policy. *International Journal for Lesson and Learning Studies*, 1(1): 85–100.

Dudley, P (2013) Teacher Learning in Lesson Study: What Interaction-Level Discourse Analysis Revealed About How Teachers Utilised Imagination, Tacit Knowledge of Teaching and Fresh Evidence of Pupils' Learning to Develop Practice Knowledge and So Enhance Their Pupils' Learning. *Teaching and Teacher Education*, 34: 107–21.

Dudley, P (2014) (ed) *Lesson Study: Professional Learning for Our Time*. London: Routledge.

DuFour, R P (1997) The School as a Learning Organization: Recommendations for School Improvement. *NASSP Bulletin*, 81(588): 81–7.

DuFour, R (2004) Schools as Learning Communities. *Educational Leadership*, 61(8): 6–11.

DuFour, R and Eaker, R (1998) *Professional Learning Communities at Work: Best Practices for Enhancing Student Achievement*. Bloomington, Ill: Solution Tree.

DuFour, R and DuFour, R (2012) *The School Leader's Guide to Professional Learning Communities at Work*. Bloomington: Solution Tree Press.

Dunn, R, Hattie, J and Bowles, T (2017) *Analysing the Growth Trajectories and Experiences of Teachers Participating in Practitioner Inquiry*. Conference paper: European Educational Research Association Annual conference. [online] Available at: www.researchgate.net/publication/319263483_Analysing_the_Growth_Trajectories_and_Experiences_of_Teachers_Participating_in_Practitioner_Inquiry_Session_Information (accessed 30 July 2019).

Education Endowment Foundation (2017) Justine Greening unveils new EEF/IEE Research Schools at the Social Mobility Summit 12 July 2017. [online] Available at https://educationendowmentfoundation.org.uk/news/justine-greening-unveils-new-eef-iee-research-schools-at-the-social-mobilit (accessed 30 July 2019).

Education Endowment Foundation (2019) London: EEF. [online] Available at: https://educationendowmentfoundation.org.uk (accessed 30 July 2019).

Egan-Simon, D and Finch, E (2018) BrewEd: Bringing Together People, Pints and Pedagogy, *Morning Star, 3 April 2018*. [online] Available at: https://morningstaronline.co.uk/article/brewed-bringing-together-people-pints-and-pedagogy (accessed 30 July 2019).

Elliott, J (1980) Implications of Classroom Research for Professional Development. In Hoyle, E and Megarr, J (eds) *Professional Development of Teachers: World Year Book of Education* (pp 308–24). London: Kogan Page.

Elliott, J (1999) *Action Research: A Framework for Self-Evaluation in Schools*. Cambridge: Cambridge Institute of Education.

Elliott, J (2004) Using Research to Improve Practice: The Notion of Evidence-based Practice. In Day, C and Sachs, J (eds) *International Handbook on the Continuing Professional Development of Teachers* (pp 264–90). Maidenhead: Open University Press.

Elliott, J (2015) Educational Action Research as the Quest for Virtue in Teaching. [online] Available at: https://ueaeprints.uea.ac.uk/53008/1/JE._Quest_for_Virtue_in_Teaching._20_11_14._Final_Dr.pdf (accessed 30 July 2019).

Emke, M (2019) Freelance language teachers' professional development on … and with … and through Twitter, Unpublished EdD thesis, Open University. [online] Available at: http://oro.open.ac.uk/60076.

Engeström, Y, Engeström, R and Vähäaho, T (1999) When the Center Does Not Hold: The Importance of Knotworking. In Chaiklin, S, Hedegaard, M and Jensen, U (eds) *Activity Theory and Social Practice: Cultural-Historical Approaches* (pp 345–74). Aarhus: Aarhus University Press.

Evans, K, Hodkinson, P, Rainbird, H and Unwin, L (2006) *Improving Workplace Learning*. Abingdon: Routledge.

Fairbanks, C M and LaGrone, D (2006) Learning Together: Constructing Knowledge in a Teacher Research Group. *Teacher Education Quarterly*, 33(3): 7–25.

Fernandez, C (2002) Learning from Japanese Approaches to Professional Development: The Case of Lesson Study. *Journal of Teacher Education*, 53(5): 393–405.

Fielding, M, Bragg, S, Craig, J, Cunningham, I, Eraut, M, Gillinson, S, Horne, M, Robinson, C and Thorp, J (2005) *Factors Influencing the Transfer of Good Practice*. Nottingham: DFES Publications.

Flyvbjerg, B (2001) *Making Social Science Matter: Why Social Inquiry Fails and How It Can Succeed Again*. Cambridge: Cambridge University Press.

Fordham, J (2017) Inquiry as a Vehicle to Change School Culture. In Poultney, V (ed) *Evidence-based Teaching in Primary Education* (pp 60–72). St Albans: Critical Publishing.

Fox, A and Bird, T (2017) The Challenge to Professionals of Using Social Media: Teachers in England Negotiating Personal–Professional Identities. *Education and Information Technologies*, 22(2): 647–75.

Fox, A and Wilson, E (2009) 'Support our networking and help us belong!': Listening to Beginning Secondary School Science Teachers. *Teachers and Teaching: Theory and Practice*, 15(6): 701–18.

Fox, A and Wilson, E (2015) Networking and the Development of Professionals: Beginning Teachers Building Social Capital. *Teaching and Teacher Education*, 47: 93–107.

Fox, A, Wilson, E and Deaney, R (2011) Beginning Teachers' Workplace Experiences: Perceptions of and Use of Support. *Vocations and Learning*, 1(1): 1–24.

Frost, D (2008) Teachers as Champions of Innovation. *Education Review*, 21(1): 13–21.

Frost, D (2013) *Teacher-Led Development Work: A Methodology for Building Professional Knowledge* (HertsCam Occasional Report 1). Cambridge: University of Cambridge Faculty of Education and HertsCam Network. [online] Available at: www.hertscam.org.uk/uploads/2/5/9/7/25979128/hertscam_occpapers_1.pdf (accessed 30 July 2019).

Frost, D (2014) *Transforming Education Through Teacher Leadership.* Herts: HertsCam Network.

Frost, D (2017) *Empowering Teachers as Agents of Change: A Non-Positional Approach to Teacher Leadership.* Herts: HertsCam Network.

Frost, D (2018) HertsCam: a Teacher-led Organisation to Support Teacher Leadership. *International Journal of Teacher Leadership* 9(1): 79–100.

Frost, D, Lightfoot, S, Hill, V and Ball, S (eds) (2018) *Teachers as Agents of Change: A Masters Programme Designed, Led and Taught by Teachers.* Letchworth Garden City: HertsCam Publications. [online] Available at: www. hertscam.org.uk/uploads/2/5/9/7/25979128/teachers_as_agents_of_change_ herts_cam_network.pdf (accessed 30 July 2019).

Fullan, M (1995) The School as a Learning Organization: Distant Dreams. *Theory Into Practice,* 34(4): 230–5.

Fuller, A and Unwin, L (2004) Expansive Learning Environments: Integrating Personal and Organisational Development. In Fuller, A and Unwin, L (eds) *Workplace Learning in Context* (pp 126–44). London: Routledge.

Gaitan, C D (2004) *Involving Latino Families in Schools: Raising Student Achievement Through Home-School Partnerships.* Thousand Oaks, CA: Corwin Press.

Gale, T (2018) What's Not To Like About RCTs in Education? In Childs, A and Menter, I (eds) *Mobilising Teacher Researchers: Challenging Educational Inequality.* London and New York: Routledge.

Gao, X A and Ko, P Y (2009) 'Learning Study' for Primary School English Teachers: A Case Story from Hong Kong. *Changing English: Studies in Culture and Education,* 16(4): 397–404.

Garrison, D R, Anderson, T and Archer, W (2010) The First Decade of the Community of Inquiry Framework: A Retrospective. *Internet and Higher Education* 13(1): 5–9.

Goldacre, B (2013a) *Building Evidence into Education.* London: HMSO.

Goldacre, B (2013b) Teachers! What Would Evidence Based Practice Look Like? London: Department for Education. [online] Available at: www.badscience.net/ 2013/03/heres-my-paper-on-evidence-and-teaching-for-the-education-minister (accessed 30 July 2019).

Goodlad, J I (1994) *Educational Renewal: Better Teachers, Better Schools*. San Francisco: Jossey-Bass Inc.

Goodnough, K (2011) Examining the Long-Term Impact of Collaborative Action Research on Teacher Identity and Practice: The Perceptions of K–12 Teachers. *Educational Action Research*, 19(1): 73–86.

Gorard, S, See, B H and Siddiqui, N (2017) *The Trials of Evidence-based Education*. London: Routledge.

Gove, M (2013) *The Importance of Teaching*. London: Department for Education. [online] Available at: www.gov.uk/government/speeches/michael-gove-speaks-about-the-importance-of-teaching (accessed 30 July 2019).

Graham, P and Ferriter, W M (2010) *Building a Professional Learning Community at Work: A Guide to the First Year*. Bloomington: Solution Tree Press.

Granovetter, M (1973) The Strength of Weak Ties. *American Journal of Sociology*, 78: 1360–80.

Granovetter, M (1983) The Strength of Weak Ties: A Network Theory Revisited. *Sociological Theory*, 1: 201–33.

Greany, T and Brown, C (2015) *Partnerships Between Teaching Schools and Universities: Research Report*. London: London Centre for Leadership in Learning, UCL Institute of Education. [online] Available at: www.researchlearningcommunities.org/uploads/2/1/6/3/21631832/_teaching_schools_and_universities_research_report.pdf (accessed 30 July 2019).

Grossman, P, Wineburg, S and Woolworth, S (2000) *What Makes Teacher Community Different from a Gathering of Teachers?* An Occasional Paper co-sponsored by Center for the Study of Teaching and Policy and Center on English Learning and Achievement, document O-00-1. Washington: Center for the Study of Teaching and Policy. [online] Available at: www.education.uw.edu/ctp/sites/default/files/ctpmail/PDFs/Community-GWW-01-2001.pdf (accessed 30 July 2019).

Gu, L and Wang, J (2003) Teachers' Growth Through Action Education, A Model of Teacher Education and Development Based on Keli. *Global Education*, 185(1): 44–9

Hagger, H and McIntyre, D (2006) *Learning Teaching from Teachers: Realising the Potential of School-based Teacher Education*. Maidenhead: Open University Press.

Hakkarainen, K, Palonen, T, Paavola, S and Lehtinen, E (2004) *Communities of Networked Expertise: Professional and Educational Perspectives.* Amsterdam: Elsevier.

Hammersley, M (2005) The Myth of Research-based Practice: The Critical Case of Educational Inquiry. *International Journal of Social Research Methodology,* 8: 317–30.

Handley, K, Sturdy, A, Fincham, R and Clark, T (2006) Within and Beyond Communities of Practice: Making Sense of Learning Through Participation, Identity and Practice. *Journal of Management Studies,* 43(3): 643–53.

Handscomb, G, Gu, Q and Varley, M (2014) *School–University Partnerships: Fulfilling the Potential. Literature Review.* London: National Co-ordinating Centre for Public Engagement. [online] Available at: www.publicengagement.ac.uk/sites/default/files/publication/supi_project_report_final.pdf (accessed 30 July 2019).

Hargreaves, A (1982) The Rhetoric of School-centred Innovation. *Journal of Curriculum Studies,* 14(3): 251–66.

Hargreaves, A (1994) *Changing Teachers, Changing Times: Teachers' Work and Culture in the Postmodern Age.* London: Cassell.

Hargreaves, A (1997) From Reform to Renewal: A New Deal for a New Age. In Hargreaves, A and Evans, R (eds) *Beyond Educational Reform: Bringing Teachers Back In* (pp 105–25). Buckingham: Open University Press.

Hargreaves, A (2000) Four Ages of Professionalism and Professional Learning. *Teachers and Teaching: Theory and Practice,* 6(2): 151–82.

Hargreaves, A (2007) Sustainable Professional Learning Communities. In Stoll, L and Louis, K S (eds) *Professional Learning Communities: Divergence, Depth and Dilemmas* (pp 181–95). Maidenhead: The Open University Press.

Hargreaves, A and Fullan, A (2012) *Professional Capital: Transforming Teaching in Every School.* London: Routledge.

Hargreaves, D H (1994) The New Professionalism: The Synthesis of Professional and Institutional Development. *Teaching and Teacher Education,* 10(4): 423–38.

Hargreaves, D H (1999) The Knowledge-Creating School. *British Journal of Educational Studies,* 47(2): 122–44.

Hargreaves, D H (2003) *Education Epidemic: Transforming Secondary Schools Through Innovation Networks.* London: HMSO.

Hargreaves, D H (2010) *Creating a Self-improving School System*. Nottingham: National College for Leadership of Schools and Children's Services.

Hargreaves, D H (2011) *A Self-improving School System: Towards Maturity*. Nottingham: National College of Teaching and Leadership.

Harris, A and Jones, M S (2017) Leading Professional Learning: Putting Teachers at the Centre. *School Leadership and Management*, 37(4): 331–3.

Hattie, J (2008) *Visible Learning: A Synthesis of Over 800 Meta-Analyses Relating to Achievement*. New York: Routledge.

Hattie, J (2012) *Visible Learning for Teachers: Maximizing Impact on Learning*. Oxon: Routledge.

Haynes, G and Lynch, S (2013) Local Partnerships: Blowing in the Wind of National Policy Changes. *British Educational Research Journal*, 39(3): 425–46.

Herbert, M (2012) Why all the Chatter About #Edchat? *District Administration*, 48(4): 4.

Higgins, S, Katsipataki, M, Kokotsaki, D, Coleman, R, Major, L E and Coe, R (2014) *The Sutton Trust-Education Endowment Foundation Teaching and Learning Toolkit*. London: Education Endowment Foundation.

Hill, R (2010) *Chain Reactions: A Thinkpiece on the Development of Chains of Schools in the English School System*. Nottingham: National College for Leadership of Schools and Children's Services. [online] Available at: https://dera.ioe.ac.uk//2070 (accessed 30 July 2019).

Holmqvist, M (2011) Teachers' Learning in a Learning Study. *Instructional Science*, 39: 497–511.

Hord, S M (1997) *Professional Learning Communities: Communities of Continuous Inquiry and Improvement*. SEDL document number: CHA-34. Texas: Southwest Educational Development Laboratory. [online] Available at: www.sedl.org/pubs/catalog/items/cha34.html (accessed 30 July 2019).

Hord, S M and Sommers, W A (2008) *Leading Professional Learning Communities: Voices from Research and Practice*. London: Corwin Press.

House of Commons (2019) A Ten-Year Plan for School and College Funding. Tenth Report of Session 2017–19. HC969. [online] Available at: https://publications.parliament.uk/pa/cm201719/cmselect/cmeduc/969/969.pdf (accessed 2 October 2019).

Huang, R, Su, H and Xu, S (2014) Developing Teachers' and Teaching Researchers' Professional Competence in Mathematics through Chinese Lesson Study. *ZDM*, 46(2): 239–51.

Husbands, C (2015) Tragedy of the Commons: How the Government Abandoned the Pursuit of Teacher Quality. London: IOE. [online] Available at: https://ioelondonblog.wordpress.com/2015/11/16/the-tragedy-of-the-commons-how-the-government-abandoned-the-pursuit-of-teacher-quality/ (accessed 30 July 2019).

Illinois State University (2019) *Carnegie Academy for the Scholarship of Teaching and Learning.* Illinois: Illinois State University. [online] Available at: https://sotl.illinoisstate.edu/resources/castl/ (accessed 30 July 2019).

Jackson, D and Temperley, J (2006) From Professional Learning Community to Networked Learning Community. Paper presented at the *International Congress for School Effectiveness and Improvement (ICSEI) Conference* 2006 Fort Lauderdale, USA, 3–6 January. [online] Available at: www.learnersfirst.net/private/wp-content/uploads/From-professional-learning-community-to-networked-learning-community.pdf (accessed 30 July 2019).

Jefferis, T and Bisschoff, T (2017) The Importance of Twitter in the Professional Development of Digitally-engaged Head Teachers. *International Studies in Educational Administration (Commonwealth Council for Educational Administration and Management (CCEAM)),* 45(2).

Johnston, M and The Educators for Collaborative Change (1997) *Contradictions in Collaboration: New Thinking on School/University Partnerships.* New York: Teachers College Press.

Katsarou, E and Tsafos, V (2008) Collaborative School Innovation Project as a Pivot for Teachers' Professional Development: The Case of Acharnes' Second Chance School in Greece. *Teacher Development,* 12(2): 125–38.

Katyal, K R and Evers, C W (2014) *Teacher Leadership: New Conceptions for Autonomous Student Learning in the Age of the Internet (Routledge Research in Education).* London: Routledge.

Katz, S and Earl, L (2010) Learning About Networked Learning Communities. *School Effectiveness and School Improvement,* 21(1): 27–51.

Katz, S, Earl, L and Jaafar, S B (2009) *Building and Connecting Learning Communities: The Power of Networks for School Improvemen*t. Thousand Oaks, CA: Corwin.

Kennedy, A (2015) What Do Professional Learning Policies Say About Purposes of Teacher Education? *Asia-Pacific Journal of Teacher Education,* 43(3): 183–94.

Kershner, R, Pedder, D and Doddington, C (2012) Professional Learning During a Schools–University Partnership Master of Education Course: Teachers'

Perspectives of Their Learning Experiences. *Teachers and Teaching: Theory and Practice*, 19(1): 33–49.

Knox, J (2013) Five Critiques of the Open Educational Resources Movement. Teaching in Higher Education, 18(8): 821–32.

Kontopoulou, K (2019) *Pre-Service Teachers' Use of Social Media for Academic Purposes*, unpublished doctoral thesis (PhD), University of Leicester.

Krammer, M, Rossmann, P, Gastager, A and Gasteiger-Klicpera, B (2018) Ways of Composing Teaching Teams and their Impact on Teachers' Perceptions About Collaboration. *European Journal of Teacher Education*, 41(4): 463–78.

Langhorst, E (2015) *Social Studies Teachers' Use of Twitter and# edchats for Collaboration*, Walden Dissertations and Doctoral Studies, Minneapolis: Walden University.

LaRocque, M, Kleiman, I and Darling, S M (2011) Parental Involvement: The Missing Link in School Achievement. *Preventing School Failure*, 55(3): 115–22.

Lave, J and Wenger, E (1991) *Situated Learning: Legitimate Peripheral Participation*. Cambridge: Cambridge University Press.

Lawrence, C A and Chong, W H (2010) Teacher Collaborative Learning through Lesson Study: Identifying Pathways for Instructional Success in a Singapore High School. *Asia Pacific Educational Review*, 11: 565–72.

Lee, J F K (2008) A Hong Kong Case of Lesson Study – Benefits and Concerns. *Teaching and Teacher Education*, 24: 1115–24.

Leijen, A and Kullasepp, K (2013) All Roads Lead to Rome: Developmental Trajectories of Student Teachers' Professional and Personal Identity Development. *Journal of Constructivist Psychology*, 26(2): 104–14.

Leithwood, K, Harris, A and Hopkins, D (2008) Seven Strong Claims about Successful School Leadership. *School Leadership and Management*, 28(1): 27–42.

Levin, B B and Rock, T C (2003) The Effects Of Collaborative Action Research On Preservice and Experienced Teacher Partners In Professional Development Schools. *Journal of Teacher Education*, 54(2): 135–49.

Levine, T H (2010) Tools for the Study and Design of Collaborative Teacher Learning: The Affordances of Different Conceptions of Teacher Community and Activity Theory. *Teacher Education Quarterly*, 37(1): 109–30.

Lewis, C (2009) What is the Nature of Knowledge Development in Lesson Study? *Educational Action Research*, 17(1): 95–110.

Lewis, C and Hurd, J (2011) *Lesson Study Step by Step: How Teacher Learning Communities Improve Instruction.* London: Heinemann.

Lewis, C, Perry, R and Murata, A (2006) How Should Research Contribute to Instructional Improvement? The Case of Lesson Study. *Educational Researcher,* 35(3): 3–14.

Lexico.com (2019) *Oxford English Dictionary.* [online] Available at: https://en.oxforddictionaries.com (accessed 30 July 2019).

Liana, L H and Ngeze, L V (2015) Online Teacher Communities of Practice: A Proposed Model to Increase Professional Development in Tanzania. *Journal of Informatics and Virtual Education,* 3(1): 22–7.

Lieberman, A and McLaughlin, M W (1992) Networks for Educational Change: Powerful and Problematic. *Phi Delta Kappan,* 74: 673–7.

Lieberman, A and Miller, L (2001) *Teacher Leadership.* Somerset, NJ: Wiley Jossey-Bass.

Lieberman, A and Miller, A (2008) *Teachers in Professional Communities: Improving Teaching and Learning (The Series on School Reform).* Columbia, Ohio: Teachers College Press.

Lieberman, A and Wood, D (2002) *Inside the National Writing Project: Connecting Network Learning and Classroom Teaching.* New York: Teachers College Press.

Lindsay, G, Muijs, D, Harris, A, Chapman, C, Arweck, E and Goodall, J (2007) *School Federations Pilot Study: 2003–2007.* Nottingham: Department for Children, Schools and Families (DCSF). [online] Available at: https://warwick.ac.uk/fac/soc/cedar/projects/completed07/federations/federationsrb30_xr253651.pdf (accessed 30 July 2019).

Little, J W (1990) The Persistence of Privacy: Autonomy and Initiative in Teachers' Professional Relations. *Teachers' College Record,* 91(4): 509–36.

Little, J W (2002) Locating Learning in Teachers' Communities of Practice: Opening Up Problems of Analysis in Records of Everyday Work. *Teaching and Teacher Education,* 18: 917–46.

Little, J W (2005) Professional Learning and School-Network Ties: Prospects for School Improvement. *Journal of Educational Change,* 6: 277–84.

Lynch, D and Smith, R (2004) When We Say 'Action', We Mean 'Business': Bringing Teachers, Lecturers, Employers and Students Together in Partnerships. In Harrison, A, Knight, B A and Walker-Gibbs, B (eds)

Educational Research: Partnerships, Initiatives and Pedagogy (pp 12–16). Flaxton: PostPressed.

Lytle, S L and Cochran-Smith, M (1992) Teacher Research as a Way of Knowing. *Harvard Educational Review*, 62(4): 447–75.

Manca, S and Ranieri, M (2017) Implications of Social Network Sites for Teaching and Learning. Where We Are and Where We Want To Go. *Education and Information Technologies*, 22(2): 605–22.

Maskit, D and Orland-Barak, L (2015) University–School Partnerships: Student Teachers' Evaluations Across Nine Partnerships in Israel. *Journal of Education for Teaching: International Research and Pedagogy*, 41(3): 285–306.

Maxwell, B, Greany, T, Aspinwall, K, Handscomb, G, Seleznyov, S and Simkins, T (2015) Approaches to research & development for 'great pedagogy'and 'great CPD' in teaching school alliances: teaching schools R&D network national themes project 2012–14.

McCormick, R, Fox, A, Carmichael, P and Procter, R (2010) *Researching and Understanding Educational Networks* (New Perspectives on Learning and Instruction series). London: Routledge.

McEwan, D, Ruissen G R, Eys, M A, Zumbo B D and Beauchamp M R (2017) The Effectiveness of Teamwork Training on Teamwork Behaviors and Team Performance: A Systematic Review and Meta-Analysis of Controlled Interventions. *PLoS ONE*, 12(1): e0169604.

McGregor, J (2004) *Studying spatiality*. Paper presented at the British Educational Research Association Annual Conference, University of Manchester, 16–18 September 2004. [online] Available at: www.leeds.ac.uk/educol/documents/00003785.htm (accessed 30 July 2019).

McLaughlin, C and Black-Hawkins, K (2004) A Schools–University Research Partnership: Understandings, Models and Complexities. *Journal of In-Service Education*, 30(2): 265–84.

McLaughlin, C and Black-Hawkins, K (2007) School–University Partnerships for Educational Research – Distinctions, Dilemmas and Challenges. *The Curriculum Journal*, 18(3): 327–41.

McLaughlin, C, Black-Hawkins, K, Brindley, S, McIntyre, D and Taber, K (2006) *Researching Schools: Stories From a Schools-University Partnership for Educational Research*. London: Routledge.

McLaughlin, C, Black-Hawkins, K and McIntyre, D (2004) *Researching Teachers, Researching Schools, Researching Networks: A Review of the Literature*. London: Routledge and University of Cambridge.

McLaughlin, C, Black-Hawkins, K, McIntyre, D with Townsend, A (2007) *Networking Practitioner Research: The Effective Use of Networks in Educational Research*. London: Taylor & Francis.

McLaughlin, M W and Talbert, J E (2001) *Professional Communities and the Work of High School Teaching*. Chicago: University of Chicago Press.

McNiff, J (2010) *Action Research for Professional Development*. London: September Books.

McNiff, J and Whitehead, J (2010) *You and Your Action Research Project*. 3rd edn. London: Routledge.

Meng, C C and Sam, L C (2011) Encouraging the Innovative Use of Geometer's Sketchpad through LS. *Creative Education*, 2(3): 236–43.

Mercer, N (1995) *The Guided Construction of Knowledge: Talk Amongst Teachers and Learners*. Clevedon: Multilingual Matters.

Muijs, D, West, M and Ainscow, M (2010) Why Network? Theoretical Perspectives on Networking. *School Effectiveness and School Improvement*, 21(1): 5–26.

Nardi, B, Whittaker, S and Schwarz, H (2000) It's Not What You Know, It's Who You Know: Work in the Information Age. *First Monday*, 5(5). [online] Available at: http://firstmonday.org/issues/issue5_5/nardi/index.html (accessed 30 July 2019).

Nardi, B, Whittaker, S and Schwarz, H (2002) NetWORKers and Their Activity in Intensional Networks. Special Issue: Activity Theory and Design. *Journal of Computer-supported Cooperative Work*, 11(1): 1–2.

National Archives (nd) *Teacher Training*. London: Department for Education. [online] Available at: www.nationalarchives.gov.uk/help-with-your-research/research-guides/teacher-training/ (accessed 30 July 2019).

Nelson, J and Campbell, C (2017) Evidence-informed Practice in Education: Meanings and Applications. *Educational Research*, 59(2): 127–35.

Nelson, R, Spence-Thomas, K and Taylor, C (2015a) *Research and Development Network: What Makes Great Pedagogy and Professional Development*. Final report DFE-RR443C. London: HMSO. [online] Available at: https://assets.publishing.service.gov.uk/government/uploads/system/uploads/attachment_data/file/406280/What_makes_great_pedagogy_and_great_professional_development_final_report.pdf (accessed 30 July 2019).

Nelson, R, Spence-Thomas, K and Taylor, C (2015b) *What Makes Great Professional Development: Research Case Studies*. Report DFE-RR443E. London: HMSO.

[online] Available at: https://assets.publishing.service.gov.uk/government/uploads/system/uploads/attachment_data/file/406282/What_makes_great_professional_development_research_case_studies.pdf (accessed 30 July 2019).

Nevo, I and Slonim-Nevo, V (2011) The Myth of Evidence-based Practice: Towards Evidence-informed Practice. *British Journal of Social Work*, 41(6): 1176–97.

Nonaka, I and Takeuchi, H (1995) *The Knowledge Creating Company*. Oxford: Oxford University Press.

Norwich, B and Ylonen, A (2013) Design-based Research to Develop the Teaching of Pupils with Moderate Learning Difficulties: Evaluating Lesson Study in Terms of Pupil, Teacher and School Outcomes. *Teaching and Teacher Education*, 34(1): 162–73.

Ofsted (2018) *Overview of Research for the Education Inspection Framework*. London: HMSO. [online] Available at: https://assets.publishing.service.gov.uk/government/uploads/system/uploads/attachment_data/file/807641/Research_for_EIF_framework_100619.pdf (accessed 30 July 2019).

O'Hara, K (2013) Does Technology Help or Hinder your Work-life Balance? *The Guardian*, 19 June 2013. [online] Available at: www.theguardian.com/careers/technology-help-hinder-work-life-balance (accessed 30 July 2019).

O'Neil, J (1995) On Schools as Learning Organizations: A Conversation with Peter Senge. *Self-Renewing Schools*, 52(7): 20–23. [online] Available at: http://patriciathinks.yolasite.com/resources/Senge.pdf (accessed 30 July 2019).

Ono, Y and Ferreira, J (2010) A Case Study of Continuing Teacher Professional Development Through Lesson Study in South Africa. *South African Journal of Education*, 30(1): 59–74.

Ono, Y, Chikamori, K and Rogan, J M (2011) Reflections on a Mutual Journey of Discovery and Growth Based on a Japanese-South African Collaboration. *Professional Development in Education*, 37: 335–52.

Ontario Ministry of Education (2010) *Collaborative Teaching Enquiry*. Capacity Building Series. Special Issue #16. Ontario: Secretariat of the Ministry of Education. [online] Available at: www.edu.gov.on.ca/eng/literacynumeracy/inspire/research/CBS_Collaborative_Teacher_Inquiry.pdf (accessed 30 July 2019).

Opfer, D and Pedder, D (2011a) Conceptualising Teacher Professional Learning. *Review of Educational Research*, 81(3): 376–407.

Opfer, V D and Pedder, D (2011b) The Lost Promise of Teacher Professional Development in England. *European Journal of Teacher Education*, 34(1): 3–24.

Organisation for Economic Co-operation and Development (OECD) (2016) What Makes a School a Learning Organisation? A Guide for Policy-makers, School Leaders and Teachers. Paris: OECD. [online] Available at: www.oecd.org/education/school/school-learning-organisation.pdf (accessed 30 July 2019).

Owen, N I, Fox, A and Bird, T M (2016) Surveying UK Teachers' Use (Not Use) and Attitudes to Social Media: A Methodological Approach. *International Journal of Research and Method in Education*, 39(2): 170–83.

Palincsar, A (1999) A Community of Practice. *Teacher Education and Special Education*, 22(4): 272–4.

Pang, M F and Ling, L M (2011) Learning Study: Helping Teachers to Use Theory, Develop Professionally, and Produce New Knowledge to be Shared. *Instructional Science*, 40(3): 589–606.

Pang, M F and Marton, F (2003) Beyond Lesson Study: Comparing Two Ways of Facilitating the Grasp of Some Economic Concepts. *Instructional Science*, 31(1): 175–94.

Pardales, M J and Girod, M (2006) Community of Inquiry: Its Past and Present Future. *Educational Philosophy and Theory*, 38(3): 299–309.

Park, S and Takahashi, S (2013) *90-Day Cycle Handbook*. Stanford: Carnegie Foundation for the Advancement of Teaching. [online] Available at: www.carnegiefoundation.org/resources/publications/90-day-cycle-handbook/ (accessed 30 July 2019).

Park, S, Henkin, A B and Egley, R (2005) Teacher Team Commitment, Teamwork and Trust: Exploring Associations. *Journal of Educational Administration*, 43(5): 462–79.

Pedder, D (2006) Organizational Conditions that Foster Successful Classroom Promotion of Learning How to Learn. *Research Papers in Education*, 21(2): 171–200.

Perry, R R and Lewis, C C (2009) What is Successful Adaptation of Lesson Study in the US? *Journal of Educational Change*, 10(4): 365–91.

Philpott, C and Poultney, V (2018) *Evidence-based Teaching: A Critical Overview for Enquiring Teachers*. St Albans: Critical Publishing.

Postholm, M B (2009) Research and Development Work: Developing Teachers as Researchers or Just Teachers? *Educational Action Research*, 17(4): 551–65.

Poultney, V (2017) *Evidence-based Teaching in Primary Education*. St Albans: Critical Publishing.

Poultney, V and Fordham, J (2017) Leading Primary School Inquiry – What Do We Need to Know About School–University Partnerships and Ways of Working. In Poultney, V (ed) *Evidence-based Teaching in Primary Education* (pp 13–23). St Albans: Critical Publishing.

Poultney, V and Fordham, J (2018) Researching Reciprocal Leadership: Using the Consciousness Quotient inventory (CQ-i) as a Pilot Methodology to Explore Leadership with the Context of a School–University Partnership. *Management in Education (Special Issue Research Methods for Educational Leadership)*, 32(1): 31–9.

Puchner, L D and Taylor, A R (2006) Lesson Study, Collaboration and Teacher Efficacy: Stories from Two School-based Math Lesson Study Groups. *Teaching and Teacher Education*, 22(7): 922–34.

Putnam, R D (1995) Bowling Alone: America's Declining Social Capital. *Journal of Democracy*, 6(1): 65–78.

Rainie, L and Wellman, B (2012) *Networked: The New Social Operating System*. Cambridge, MA: MIT Press.

Rajagopal, K, Joosten Brinke, D, Van Bruggen, J and Sloep, P B (2012) Understanding Personal Learning Networks: Their Structure, Content and the Networking Skills Needed to Optimally Use Them. *First Monday*, 17(1–2). [online] Available at: http://firstmonday.org/ojs/index.php/fm/article/view/3559/3131 (accessed 30 July 2019).

researchED (nd) *researchED*. [online] Available at: https://researched.org.uk (accessed 2 October 2019).

Research School Network (nd) *Research School*. [online] Available at: https://researchschool.org.uk (accessed 2 October 2019).

Richardson, W and Mancabelli, R (2011) *Personal Learning Networks: Using the Power of Connections to Transform Education*. Bloomington, In: Solution Tree Press.

Robinson, N and Leikin, R (2012) One Teacher, Two Lessons: The Lesson Study Process. *International Journal of Science and Mathematics Education*, 10(1): 139–61.

Robson, J (2016) Engagement in Structured Social Space: An Investigation of Teachers' Online Peer-to-Peer Interaction. *Learning, Media and Technology*, 41(1): 119–39.

Rosenholtz, S J (1989) *Teacher's Workplace: The Social Organisation of Schools*. New York: Longman.

RSA Teaching School Alliance (2019a) *Enquiry Fellowship*. [online] Available at: www.rsaacademiesteachingschool.org.uk/what-we-offer/enquiry-fellowship (accessed 2 October 2019).

RSA Teaching School Alliance (2019b) *Research and Development*. [online] Available at: www.rsaacademiesteachingschool.org.uk/researchanddevelopment (accessed 2 October 2019).

RSA Teaching School Alliance (2019c) Research Enquiries from the RSA Teacher Trainees . [online] Available at: www.rsaacademies.org.uk/research-enquiries-rsa-teacher-trainees (accessed 2 October 2019).

RSA Teaching School Alliance (2019d) Research Rich Schools Project . [online] Available at: www.rsaacademies.org.uk/projects/research-rich-schools (accessed 2 October 2019).

Rycroft-Malone, J O (2008) Evidence-informed Practice: From Individual to Context. *Journal of Nursing Management*, 16(4): 404–8.

Sachs, J (2003) *The Activist Teaching Profession (Professional Learning)*. Buckingham: Open University Press.

Sachs, J (2016) Teacher Professionalism: Why Are We Still Talking About It? *Teachers and Teaching: Theory and Practice*, 22(4): 413–25.

Sagor, R (1992) *How to Conduct Collaborative Action Research*. Alexandria, VA: Association for Supervision and Curriculum Development.

Sahlberg, P (2010) The Secret to Finland's Success: Educating Teachers. *Stanford Center for Opportunity Policy in Education*, 2: 1–8. [online] Available at: www.nnstoy.org/download/preparation/Secret%20to%20Finland's%20Success%20-%20Education%20Teachers.pdf (accessed 30 July 2019).

Saito, E (2012) Key Issues of Lesson Study in Japan and the United States: A Literature Review. *Professional Development in Education*, 38(5): 777–89.

Saito, E and Sato, M (2012) Lesson Study as an Instrument for School Reform: A Case of Japanese Practices. *Management in Education*, 26(4): 181–6.

Saito, E, Hawe, P, Hadiprawiroc, S and Empedhe, S (2008) Initiating Education Reform Through Lesson Study at a University in Indonesia. *Educational Action Research*, 16(3): 391–406.

Saito, E, Khong, T D H and Tsukui, A (2012) Why is School Reform Sustained Even After a Project? A Case Study of Bac Giang Province, Vietnam. *Journal of Educational Change*, 13(1): 259–87.

Salomon, G and Perkins, D N (1998) Chapter 1: Individual and Social Aspects of Learning. *Review of Research in Education*, 23(1): 1–24.

Saunders, L (2015) Evidence and Teaching: A Question of Trust? In Brown, C and Bennett, R (eds) *Leading the Use of Research and Evidence in Schools* (pp 39–52). London: IOE Press.

Schlager, M S, Farooq, U, Fusco, J, Schank, P and Dwyer, N (2009) Analyzing Online Teacher Networks: Cyber Networks Require Cyber Research Tools. *Journal of Teacher Education*, 60: 86–100.

Schön, D (1984) *The Reflective Practitioner: How Professionals Think in Action*. New York: Basic Books.

Schwille, J, Dembele, M and Schuburt, J (2007) *Global Perspectives on Teacher Learning: Improving Policy and Practice*. Paris: IIEP-UNESCO.

Sebba, J, Kent, P and Tregenza, J (2012) *Joint Practice Development: What Does The Evidence Suggest Are Effective Approaches?* [online] Available at: www.gov.uk/government/publications/joint-practice-development-what-does-the-evidence-suggest-are-effective-approaches (accessed 30 July 2019).

See, B H, Gorard, S and Siddiqui, N (2016) Teachers' Use of Research Evidence in Practice: A Pilot Study of Feedback to Enhance Learning. *Educational Research*, 58(1): 56–72.

Senge, P M (1990) *The Fifth Discipline: The Art and Practice of the Learning Organisation*. New York: Currency-DoubleDay.

Servage, L (2008) Critical Transformative Practices in Professional Learning Communities. *Teacher Education Quarterly*, 35(1): 63–77.

Servage, L (2009) Who Is the 'Professional' in a Professional Learning Community? An Exploration of Teacher Professionalism in Collaborative Professional Development Settings. *Canadian Journal of Education*, 32(1): 149–71.

Sfard, A (1998) On Two Metaphors for Learning and the Dangers of Choosing Just One. *Educational Researcher*, 27(2): 4–13.

Sims, L and Walsh, D (2009) Lesson Study with Preservice Teachers: Lessons from Lessons. *Teaching and Teacher Education*, 25: 724–33.

Slavin, R E (2004) Education Research Can and Must Address 'What Works' Questions. *Educational Researcher*, 33(1): 27–8.

Smedley, L (2001) Impediments to Partnership: A Literature Review of School–University Links. *Teachers and Teaching: Theory and Practice*, 7(2): 189–209.

Smythe, J (1991) International Perspectives on Teacher Collegiality: A Labour Process, Discussion Based on the Concept of Teachers' Work. *British Journal of the Sociology of Education*, 12(3): 323–46.

Snow, J and Marshall, D (2010) The More Things Change ... Re-discovering Stubbornness and Persistence in School–University Collaborations. *Journal of Curriculum Studies*, 34(4): 481–94.

Somekh, B (2010) The Collaborative Action Research Network: 30 Years of Agency in Developing Educational Action Research. *Educational Action Research*, 18(1): 103–21.

Spielman, A (2019) *Education Inspection Framework.* [online] Available at: www.gov.uk/government/news/chief-inspector-sets-out-vision-for-new-education-inspection-framework (accessed 30 July 2019).

Stenhouse, L (1968) The Humanities Curriculum Project. *Journal of Curriculum Studies*, 1(1): 26–33. [online] Available at: www.tandfonline.com/doi/abs/10.1080/0022027680010103 (accessed 30 July 2019).

Stenhouse, L (1975) *An Introduction to Curriculum Research and Development.* London: Heinemann Educational Books.

Stenhouse, L (1981) What Counts as Research? *British Journal of Educational Studies,* 29(2): 103–14.

Stenhouse, L (1983) *Authority, Education and Emancipation: A Collection of Papers by Lawrence Stenhouse.* London: Heinemann Educational Books Ltd.

Stigler, J W and Hiebert, J (1999) *The Teaching Gap: Best Ideas from the World's Teachers for Improving Education in the Classroom.* New York: The Free Press.

Stoll, L (2010) Connecting Learning Communities: Capacity Building for Systemic Change. In Hargreaves, A, Lieberman, A, Fullan, M and Hopkins, D (eds) *Second International Handbook of Educational Change. Springer International Handbooks of Education,* Volume 23 (pp 469–84). Dordrecht: Springer.

Stoll, L, Bolam, R, McMahon, A, Wallace, M and Thomas, S (2006) Professional Learning Communities: A Review of the Literature. *Journal of Educational Change,* 7(1): 221–58.

Stoll, L, Brown, C, Spence-Thomas, K and Taylor, C (2018) Teacher Leadership Within and Across Professional Learning Communities. In Harris, A, Jones, M and Huffman, J (eds) *Teachers Leading Educational Reform: The Power of Professional Learning Communities* (pp 51–71). London: Routledge.

Stoll, L, Halbert, J and Kaser, L (2012a) Deepening Learning in School-to-School Networks. In Day, C (ed) *The Routledge International Handbook of Teacher and School Development* (pp 493–505). London: Routledge.

Stoll, L, Harris, A and Handscomb, G (2012b) *Great Professional Development Which Leads to Great Pedagogy: Nine Claims From Research*. Nottingham: National College for Teaching and Leadership. [online] Available at: https://assets.publishing.service.gov.uk/government/uploads/system/uploads/attachment_data/file/335707/Great-professional-development-which-leads-to-great-pedagogy-nine-claims-from-research.pdf (accessed 30 July 2019).

Stoll, L and Louis, K S (eds) (2007) *Professional Learning Communities: Divergence, Depth and Dilemmas*. Maidenhead: The Open University Press.

Sutton Trust (2012–2018) *The Sutton Trust*. [online] Available at: www.suttontrust.com (accessed 30 July 2019).

Swap, S M (1993) *Developing Home-School Partnerships: From Concepts to Practice*. New York: Teachers College Press.

Takahashi, A (2014) The Role of the Knowledgeable Other in LS: Examining the Final Comments of Experienced LS Practitioners. *Mathematics Teacher Education and Development*, 16(1): n1.

Talbert, J E (2010) Professional Learning Communities at the Crossroads: How Systems Hinder or Engender Change. *Second International Handbook of Educational Change*. Dordrecht: Springer.

Taylor, A (2008) Developing Understanding About Learning to Teach in a University–Schools Partnership in England. *British Educational Research Journal*, 34(1): 63–90.

Teacher Education Advancement Network (TEAN) (2019a) *Teaching: A Masters Profession*. [online] Available at: www.cumbria.ac.uk/research/enterprise/tean/teachers-and-educators-storehouse/teaching-a-masters-profession/ (accessed 30 July 2019).

Teacher Education Advancement Network (TEAN) (2019b) *Masters Route to Teacher Professionalism*. [online] Available at: www.cumbria.ac.uk/research/enterprise/tean/teachers-and-educators-storehouse/masters-route-teacher-professionalism/ (accessed 30 July 2019).

The Brock University and Halton Region Collaborative Teacher Enquiry team (2018) A Collaborative Teacher Enquiry into Makerspace: University and Schools Learn Together, Tips from the Experts, 11 April 2018, Knowledge Network for Applied Education Research (KNAER-RECRAE). [online] Available at: www.knaer-recrae.ca/index.php/knowledge-hub/kmb-blog/9-tips-from-the-experts/383-a-collaborative-teacher-inquiry-into-makerspace-university-schools-learn-together (accessed 30 July 2019).

The Secret Teacher (2018) Secret Teacher: Social Media Makes It Impossible to Switch Off From Work, *The Guardian: Teacher Network,* 24 February 2018. [online] Available at: www.theguardian.com/teacher-network/2018/feb/24/secret-teacher-social-media-mind-work-life-balance-stress (accessed 30 July 2019).

Thompson, S and Thompson, N (2008) *The Critically Reflective Practitioner.* Basingstoke: Palgrave MacMillan.

Townsend, A (2019) Situating Partnership Activity, An Activity Theory Inspired Analysis of School-to-School Inquiry Networks. *Cogent Education,* 6(1): 1576424. [online] Available at: https://doi.org/10.1080/2331186X.2019.1576424 (accessed 30 July 2019).

Tregenza, J, Sebba, J and Kent, P (2012) *Powerful Professional Learning: A School Leader's Guide to Joint Practice Development.* Nottingham: National College for Teaching and Leadership. [online] Available at: https://assets.publishing.service.gov.uk/government/uploads/system/uploads/attachment_data/file/329717/powerful-professional-learning-a-school-leaders-guide-to-joint-practice-development.pdf (accessed 30 July 2019).

Tsui, A and Law, D (2007) Learning as Boundary-Crossing in School–University Partnership. *Teaching and Teacher Education*, 23(8): 1289–301.

Tsui, A B M and Wong, J L N (2010) In Search of a Third Space: Teacher Development in Mainland China. In Chan, C K K and Rao, N (eds) *Revisiting the Chinese Learner, Changing Contexts, Changing Education* (pp 281–311). Hong Kong: Comparative Education Research Centre/Springer Academic Publishers.

University of East Anglia (2019) *Classroom Action Research Network.* Website. Norwich: University of East Anglia. [online] Available at: www.uea.ac.uk/education/research/care/case-studies/classroom-action-research-network (accessed 30 July 2019).

Van Swet, J, Armstrong, A C and Lloyd, C (2012) International Collaboration as a Patchwork Quilt: Experiences of Developing Collaborative Practice and Research in an International Masters Programme. *Professional Development in Education*, 38(4): 647–61.

Vescio, V, Ross, D and Adams, A (2008) A Review of Research on the Impact of Professional Learning Communities on Teaching Practice and Student learning. *Teaching and Teacher Education*, 24(1): 80–91.

Veugelers, W and O'Hair, M J (eds) (2005) *Network Learning for Educational Change.* Maidenhead: Open University Press.

Villegas-Reimers, E (2003) *Teacher Professional Development: An International Review of the Literature*. Paris: IIEP-UNESCO.

Vygotsky, L S (1987) *Mind in Society: The Development of Higher Psychological Processes*. Massachusetts and London: Harvard University Press.

Waak, S (2019) *Visible Learning*. [online] Available at: https://visible-learning.org (accessed 30 July 2019).

Walsh, C S, Bradshaw, P and Twining, P (2011) e-Learning Through Collaborative Teacher Professional Development in Primary and Secondary Schools in England. *IADIS International Conference e-Learning July 2011*. [online] Available at: http://oro.open.ac.uk/29180 (accessed 2 October 2019).

Waterhouse, J, McLellan, R, McLaughlin, C and Morgan, B (2013) Powerful Partnership in a School–University Research Collaboration: Evidence-based Reflection as a Key to Creative Action. In Stern, T, Rauch, F, Schuster, A and Townsend, A (eds) *Action Research, Innovation and Change: International and Interdisciplinary Perspectives* (pp 101–19). London: Routledge.

Watson, C (2014) Effective Professional Learning Communities? The Possibilities for Teachers as Agents of Change in Schools. *British Educational Research Journal*, 40(1): 18–29.

Watson, C and Drew, V (2017) Enacting Educational Partnership: Collective Identity, Decision-making (and the Importance of Muffin Chat). *School Leadership and Management*, 37(1–2): 3–18.

Wenger, E (1998) *Communities of Practice: Learning, Meaning, and Identity*. Cambridge: Cambridge University Press.

Wenger, E and Snyder, W (2000) Communities of Practice: The Organizational Frontier. *Harvard Business Review*, 78(1): 139–46.

Wenger, E, McDermott, R A and Snyder, W (2002) *Cultivating Communities of Practice: A Guide to Managing Knowledge*. Cambridge, MA: Harvard Business Press.

Wenger-Trayner, E, Fenton-O'Creevy, M, Hutchinson, S, Kubiak, C and Wenger-Trayner, B (2015) *Learning in Landscapes of Practice: Boundaries, Identity and Knowledgeability in Practice-Based Learning*. London: Routledge.

Whittaker, F (2016) Government Scraps Prescriptive Home–School Agreements to Cut Red Tape, *Schools Week*, 5 January 2016. [online] Available at:

https://schoolsweek.co.uk/government-scraps-prescriptive-home-school-agreements-in-bid-to-cut-red-tape (accessed 30 July 2019).

Woodbury, G and Kuhnke, J (2014) Evidence-based vs. Evidence-informed Practice: What Is the Difference? *ET Research 101*, 12(1): 26–9.

Woods, P A, Levacic, R, Evans, J, Castle, F, Glatter, R and Cooper, D (2006) *Diversity and Collaboration? Diversity Pathfinders Evaluation. Report 826.* London: Department for Education and Skills.

Wrigley, T (2018) 'Evidence' and the EEF Toolkit: Reliable Science or a Blunt Set of Tools? *British Educational Research Association.* [online] Available at: www.bera.ac.uk/blog/evidence-and-the-eef-toolkit-reliable-science-or-a-blunt-set-of-tools (accessed 8 October 2019).

Wyse, D, Brown, C, Oliver, S and Poblete, X (2018) *The BERA Close-to-Practice Research Project: Research Report.* London: BERA. [online] Available at: www.bera.ac.uk/researchersresources/publications/bera-statement-on-close-to-practice-research (accessed 30 July 2019).

Xu, H (2016) When the Water Flows, a Channel Is Formed: Professional Learning and Practice Innovation Through District Research Lesson Study in the Context of China's New Curriculum Reform. Unpublished PhD Dissertation. [online] Available at: https://ethos.bl.uk/OrderDetails.do?did=1&uin=uk.bl.ethos.677438 (accessed 2 October 2019).

Xu, H and Pedder, D (2014) Lesson Study: An International Literature Review. In Dudley, P (ed) *Lesson Study: Professional Learning for our time* (pp 29–58). London: Routledge.

Yamagata-Lynch, I C and Smaldino, S (2007) Using Activity Theory to Evaluate and Improve K-12 School and University Partnerships. *Evaluation and Program Planning*, 30(4): 364–80.

Young, V F (2006) Teachers' Use of Data: Loose Coupling, Agenda Setting, and Team Norms. *American Journal of Education*, 112(4): 521–48.

Zeichner, K (2010) Rethinking the Connection Between Campus Courses and Field Experiences in College and University-based Teacher Education. *Journal of Teacher Education,* 61(1–2): 89–99.

Zhang, L (2006) *Does Public Funding for Higher Education Matter?* ILR Collection Working Papers 149. Ithaca, NY: Cornell University. [online] Available at: https://digitalcommons.ilr.cornell.edu/workingpapers/149 (accessed 30 July 2019).

Index

Page numbers in **bold** and *italics* refer to tables and figures, respectively.

Printed in the United States
by Baker & Taylor Publisher Services